100
THINGS
TO DO IN
MEMPHIS
BEFORE YOU
DIE

100 THINGS TO DO IN MEMPHIS BEFORE YOU DIE

SAMANTHA CRESPO

REEDY PRESS
St. Louis, Missouri

To Pepo and Nina,
my dear research assistants

Reedy Press
PO Box 5131
St. Louis, MO 63139, USA
www.reedypress.com

Library of Congress Control Number: 2014937657

ISBN: 978-1-935806-80-6

Design by Jill Halpin

Printed in the United States of America
14 15 16 17 18   5 4 3 2 1

Cover photo: St. Blues Guitar Workshop

Please note that websites, phone numbers, addresses, and company names are subject to change or cancellation. We did our best to relay the most accurate information available, but due to circumstances beyond our control, please do not hold us liable for misinformation. When exploring new destinations, please do your homework before you go.

For more information, or to share your stories, please visit @SamCrespo.

CONTENTS

• •

PREFACE

I wrote this book for two audiences:

1. Travelers worldwide who come, or dream of coming, to Memphis in search of its spell; and

2. Memphians in need of rekindling their love affair with the city, or of experiencing it in new or unexpected ways.

To travelers: Welcome. I'm always warmed by the torch you carry for this city. You should know that as a traveler myself, my desire is to understand a place and ultimately, intimately, get to know it by seeking its most authentic experiences. That doesn't mean I shun the obvious attractions; it means I mix them in with spots the locals let me in on. For this book, it means you're getting a mix, too—the obvious and less obvious. How deep you venture into the mix might depend on whether you're a first-time or repeat visitor, and what your travel personality is.

To Memphians: Come play with me a game I like to call "Tourist in Our Own Town." The objective is to quash excuses. I understand them: You moved to the 'burbs and downtown isn't right around the corner anymore. You've been there/done that, and anyway, you don't have an out-of-towner on your arm. You've always wanted to do (insert wish here) but (insert excuse here). Let this book be your motivator to get out and do those things: some old, some new, some you've always wanted to do.

Now, let's get tactical:

- Always call ahead, if you can, to establishments. Though addresses, phone numbers, websites, dates, and hours were accurate immediately prior to publication, things change.

- As you read, you'll notice I've loosely organized suggestions for you by theme and neighborhood. I've also grouped some of the entries into itineraries and seasonal suggestions beginning on page 123.

And, as many suggestions as I've included over these hundred entries, I've left at least as many out. Follow me @SamCrespo for more discoveries, and to tell me about yours.

Samantha Crespo
March 2014

100

THINGS
TO DO IN
MEMPHIS
BEFORE YOU
DIE

COME HOME, MUSIC LOVER
MEMPHIS JONES

You might know a lot about Memphis music. Memphis Jones knows more. And so his show goes at B.B. King's Beale Street Blues Club—a music history lesson set to . . . well, you know. As Jones's narrative weaves through backstories and feels down the fringes of the city's musical patchwork, you're reminded that the threads of world music unraveled from Beale Street. Jones's set list, ranging from the Box Tops' "The Letter" to Mahalia Jackson's "Move On Up a Little Higher," won't let you forget it. Bonus: Jones pulls the early shift at B.B. King's (5:30–8 p.m. usually once or twice a week) and keeps the volume low, presenting the perfect Memphis music primer for junior rockers.

B.B. King's Blues Club, 143 Beale St., 901-524-5464, bbkingclubs.com
Follow Memphis Jones @MemphisJones

LEARN YOUR PLAIN JANE FROM YOUR PROZAC
MUDDY'S BAKE SHOP

Kat Gordon and her team at Muddy's Bake Shop may not know you, but they bake for you like they love you. That explains why locals considered it the best.news.EVER. when Muddy's announced plans to open a second location in 2014. Maybe offering two locations will make the lines at this from-scratch bakery shorter. Maybe it won't. I say it doesn't matter: File in with the devotees and employ a conversation starter such as, "Are you a Plain Jane or a Prozac?" (That's Muddy's-speak for vanilla-on-vanilla and chocolate-on-chocolate cupcakes.) Then determine which item you'll pledge your allegiance to. The Chocolate Chunka Burnin' Love, a double-chocolate cookie spiked with cayenne and cinnamon sugar? Gordon's personal favorite: a slice of Nancy's Boy coconut chess pie with a cup of Muddy's signature Gnome Sweet Gnome coffee?

Muddy's Bake Shop, 5101 Sanderlin Ave., #114,
901-683-8844, muddysbakeshop.com *Closed Sunday*

Muddy's Midtown, 585 S. Cooper St., muddysbakeshop.com

What's that?
You need "real food" first?
Turn the page.

'CUE UP SOME GRUB
MY TOP THREE BARBECUE SPOTS

For a food that brings people together, barbecue as a conversation topic can be downright polarizing—especially in a 'cue capital like Memphis, where we're spoiled from our shoulders to our butts, and hotly opinionated. But *I'm* writing this book, so I'm laying out *my* top three. Let the debates commence.

Central BBQ

Hit the Central Avenue location for the patio and the pulled pork (or chicken or beef or turkey) nachos. Drizzle your basket with the molasses-based sauce to achieve the ultimate salty/spicy/sweet trifecta. Avoid lines by going slightly before or after peak lunch and dinner times.

2249 Central Ave., 901-272-9377, cbqmemphis.com

Cozy Corner

You're not here for the atmosphere; you're here for the sliced pork sandwich, stacked with slaw on a sesame seed roll and sauced hot for a slow burn. Order it mild if you must.

745 N. Parkway, 901-527-9158,
cozycornerbbq.com *Closed Sunday and Monday*

The Rendezvous

For me, it's not about the dry-rubbed ribs. It's about the exercise of finding the restaurant in the alley where it's been since 1948 and talking to the waiters who've worked here almost as long. Also, I'm pretty sure that balancing your barbecue intake with Mama's Real Greek Salad voids all sins.

52 S. 2nd St., 901-523-2746, hogsfly.com *Closed Sunday and Monday*

PICK THESE MARKETS CLEAN
MUST-SHOP FARMERS' MARKETS

Throw a squash in Memphis and you're liable to hit a farmers' market. Following are my favorites; let your shopping list and location within the city help you decide which one(s) you'll scavenge. Don't forget the farmers' market at Memphis Botanic Garden, page 26.

Bobby Lanier Farm Park Market

Buy your fruits, veggies, fresh bread, even fresh chips and guacamole from Las Delicias Tortilleria; then meander through the community garden, past the chicken yard and the Kiddie Corral (stocked with hula hoops and stick ponies) to the food trucks.

Market sets up behind Germantown Elementary School, 2730 Cross Country Dr., Germantown, germantown-tn.gov
Open June through August, late Thursday afternoons.

Cooper-Young Community Farmers' Market

What the blacktop surroundings lack in ambience, this market makes up for in a close-knit vibe. Go for a steamy cup of Memphis-roasted J. Brooks coffee, free when you purchase a bag of whole-bean or ground, and monthly first-Saturday artisan fairs.

Market sets up in the parking lot of First Congregational Church, 1000 S. Cooper St. (at the corner of Walker Avenue and South Cooper Street), cycfarmersmarket.org
Open April through October, Saturday, 8 a.m.–1 p.m.; November through March, Saturday, 9 a.m.–1 p.m.

Memphis Farmers' Market

Seventy-five-plus regional vendors from Apothecary Fairy botanic soap to Bonnie Blue Farm goat cheese, rounded out by food trucks and weekly programming: live music, cooking demos, kids' activities, and the like.

Market sets up at the Central Station Pavilion at G.E. Patterson Avenue and South Front Street, memphisfarmersmarket.org
Open April through October, Saturday, 7 a.m.–1 p.m.

FEEL GOOD ABOUT YOUR FOOD
TROLLEY STOP MARKET

I struggle to pinpoint what I relish most about Trolley Stop Market. It's the sum of the flowery, vinyl tablecloths, the craveable menu honoring local farmers and producers, including owners Keith and Jill Forrester, and the artful/edible market that feels like Etsy brought to life. Arrive hungry and order the farm-fresh lunch special or a local beef burger, or a pizza for the table. Scratch-made dough layered with your choice of grilled meats and a bounty of veggies make Trolley Stop pizzas your own; weeknight dinner specials, Saturday brunch, regional beers and a kids' menu make the restaurant my all-around winner. Save room for cake, and pick up a handcrafted something on your way out . . . Melissa Bridgman's pottery always makes me smile.

704 Madison Ave., 901-526-1361, trolleystopmarket.com *Closed Sunday*

PICK YOUR OWN
JONES ORCHARD

In season, I can buy my peaches from Jones Orchard at any of the farmers' markets on pages 8 and 9. But at least once a year, I pick my own. Sure, it saves a few dollars, but I like driving all rumbly-tumbly along the gravel roads into the orchard, where the peaches blaze like fireballs in the trees and beg to be eaten right there, juice dribbling onto the grass. Jones operates three pick-your-own orchards just outside Memphis in Millington and publishes a handy ripening calendar online so you'll know when to go for peaches or strawberries or nectarines or plums or apples or what have you. Bonus: The Highway 51 location stocks a small market with fresh produce and Juanita Jones's jams, jellies, preserves, and baked goods. Her chocolate fudge pie is an ooey-gooey revelation.

7170 Hwy. 51 N., Millington, 901-873-3150,
jonesorchard.com *Closed Sunday*

DRINK THE WATER
(It's What Makes the Beer Taste So Good.)
BOSCOS SQUARED AND GHOST RIVER BREWING

Beneath Beale and Elvis Presley Boulevard and all those other Memphis streets you're beating, four natural aquifers flow with pure water. Beer is 95 percent water. How good is beer brewed in Memphis? *So* good.

Start at Boscos Squared, the second Memphis-area location of Tennessee's first brew pub. You're likely to find eight selections brewed onsite and on tap; order the sampler for a taste of each, or time your visit with happy hour for dollar-off pints, Monday through Friday, 3:30–6:30 p.m.

You should also taste what Ghost River's brewing (that's the side project of Boscos' owners that grew into its own outfit, with its own recipes, in 2008). Buy a growler straight off the loading dock or look for the craft label in restaurants, grocery stores, and growler-filling stations around town. Naturally, head brewer Jimmy Randall recommends Ghost River's Golden Ale: "It's still a beer. But it really lets the water shine for what it is."

Boscos Squared, 2120 Madison Ave., 901-432-2222, boscosbeer.com

Ghost River Brewing, 827 S. Main St., 901-278-0140, ghostriverbrewing.com *Closed Sunday*

THE EASIEST BEER RUN YOU'LL EVER MAKE
COOPER-YOUNG REGIONAL BEERFEST

How convenient would it be if you could sample all of Memphis's craft beers in one place? What if regional craft beers from Lexington, Little Rock, Nashville, New Orleans, and St. Louis were there, too? And what if the tastings were unlimited? Bookmark Cooper-Young Regional Beerfest, annually in October, when 30 local and regional craft brewers will serve you 'til the festival taps out. You'll need to be 21 and have a wristband; at the festival, the wristband gets you a mug—you know what that's for. And for goodness' sake, buy your wristband in advance. There's nothing that puts a tear in my beer like seeing a fellow appreciator turned away once this thing sells out.

beerfest.cooperyoung.org

SAMPLE THE REVOLUTION
MEMPHIS CRAFT BEERS

Like any city with decent taste, Memphis is busy birthing craft breweries. You met the pioneers on page 12; now meet the newbies. As each one grows, kick back with any one of their brews, available in restaurants and bars, some in grocery stores, too, around town. Check each brewery's website or social media feeds for available locations.

High Cotton Brewing Co.

High Cotton's lemony, peppery Saison is always on my mind. Expect a tap room and tours in 2014.

598 Monroe Ave., 901-543-4444, highcottonbrewing.com

Memphis Made Brewing Co.

Stuck in a beer rut? Memphis Made shakes you out of it by changing its brews with the seasons. If you're lucky, your favorites will come back around. And so I pine for the return of my winter crush: Lights Out, a dark and sweet wit bier.

901-207-5343, memphismadebrewing.com

Wiseacre Brewing Co.

Here's a tap room for you (Memphis's first): a wood and steel hang that fits right into the art-meets-industry aura of Broad Avenue, page 68. Sampler glasses give you a taste of any, or all, of the seven to 10 beers on draft, including high-gravity selections.

2783 Broad Ave., wiseacrebrew.com *Closed Sunday through Wednesday*

TOAST TO THE MUSIC
OLD MILLINGTON WINERY

West Tennessee is no Wine Country. But Millington, just minutes outside Memphis where the city streets give way to walls of green foliage and yards read like farms, claims Old Millington Winery. Owner Perry Welch skews the profile sweet for Southern tastes at his small-batch shop where every bottle costs around $10. Breeze by for a tasting, or do as I do and wait for a Sunday afternoon when Welch hosts live music outside the winery, April through June, and again in September and October. For $5, you can enter with a cooler or picnic basket, blankets and chairs, even your own beer, and buy wine by the bottle onsite. I think the Delta Blush pairs beautifully with a sunny afternoon and live music.

6748 Old Millington Rd., Millington, 901-873-4114, oldmillingtonwinery.com *Closed Monday and Tuesday*

IN THE NEIGHBORHOOD:
SIT ON THE PORCH
AT SHELBY FOREST GENERAL STORE

Count on Shelby Forest General Store for taxidermy décor and the essentials: ice cream, beer, disc golf supplies, and short-order standards so messy, they beg to be eaten outside. Lucky you, the store's front porch lines up picnic tables for lunching and people-watching, particularly the yin-yang of motorcyclists and road bikers heading for the shady hills of neighboring Meeman-Shelby Forest State Park, page 80. When the weather's kind, usually March through May and again Labor Day through November, the front porch hosts live music, too. Listen for bluegrass jams, acoustic bits, and the like Saturday, noon–3 p.m.; Sunday, 1–4 p.m. If you're unsure what to order, the cheeseburger all the way—with a wad of napkins—is solid.

7729 Benjestown Rd., Millington, 901-876-5770,
shelbyforestgeneralstore.com

DIVE IN
BARS WITH BEER, MUSIC, AND MORE

In the milieu of Memphis dive bars, you might find pool tables or a jukebox, karaoke, or local and touring musicians who'll talk to you while they're packing their equipment in and out. It's a world of markered bathrooms and low to no light that cops the occasional cameo in a Craig Brewer production. Memphians embrace their dive bars like a stranger grips you in a drunken hug. When you really want to lose yourself among the locals, dive in.

Buccaneer Lounge

Small, dark, and smoky for those nights you want to cozy up to a bar and occasional DJ or live music, like Devil Train on Monday evenings.

1368 Monroe Ave., 901-278-0909, facebook.com/BuccaneerLounge

Hi-Tone Café

Music comes first at the Hi-Tone, where regular bookings shuffle variety through town—like the Dick Dale-to-Of Montreal kind of variety—and there's always room on stage for hometowners.

412–414 N. Cleveland St., 901-278-8663, hitonememphis.com

The P & H Café

You'll know it by the mural outside. Come in for the selection of beer and burgers; stay for basketball on the flat screens, electronic darts, and occasional live music, or to stare at the caricatured ceiling.

1532 Madison Ave., 901-726-0906, pandhcafe.com *Closed Sunday*

The Poplar Lounge

Music's the thing here, too, and though a patio gives room to breathe, I prefer stuffing into the bar where bands shoehorn themselves into the homey performance space.

2586 Poplar Ave., 901-324-6550, thepoplarlounge.com

HAUNT EARNESTINE & HAZEL'S

It's an ex-brothel! It's haunted! The Rolling Stones wrote songs about it! *Esquire* said you should go! Get to Earnestine & Hazel's and tell me why *you* treasure the place. Is it the jukebox that rocks seamlessly from Booker T. & the MGs to Talking Heads? The peeling paint and soft-spotted stairs that signal this building's been around? The upstairs rooms scattered with cast-off furniture and ancient electronics? The open windows that frame that frozen-in-time feel of South Main Street? Nate the barkeep? The soul burgers and beer ('cause that's all that's on the menu)? These are my reasons. What are yours?

531 S. Main St., 901-523-9754, earnestineandhazelsjukejoint.com

Tip

Arrive early for a solitary experience, particularly if you want to appreciate the singularity of the upstairs. To feel the energy of the crowd, show late—say 11 p.m. on a Friday or Saturday. For live jazz, stop in on a Sunday, 7–10 p.m.

ONE FOR THE KIDS
THE CHILDREN'S MUSEUM OF MEMPHIS

Do not pass the Children's Museum of Memphis with children unless you're prepared to stop. The technicolor exterior, intensified by the 2013 addition of a splash pad, grabs kids' attention like a paper wand grabs spun sugar. Inside, they can scale a mini rock-climbing wall, sit in the cockpit of a FedEx plane, check out traveling exhibits, and if they're no older than 4, play in a designated area set to triple in size in 2014.

2525 Central Ave., 901-458-2678, cmom.com

Tip

The splash pad, open Memorial
Day through Labor Day, weather
permitting, requires separate admission
($10 per person; accompanying adults pay,
too) from the Children's Museum ($12 per
person). If you're planning to do both, buy the
$20 combo ticket. Better yet? Pack a picnic.
The museum staffs a deli and snack bar,
but you're welcome to bring your own
to the picnic areas surrounding
the splash pad.

ONE FOR THE KIDS YOU'LL LIKE, TOO
(Mama's a Head-Banger Edition)
MEMPHIS ROCK-N-ROMP

I adore my daughter and doing anything with her. Yet there are days I'd rather bang my head than do conventional kiddie-stuff. That's where Rock-n-Romp comes in: staging local musicians all ages can appreciate in a family-friendly setting. The rules are simple: Don't come without a kid. Give $5 or more per adult at the "door"; under-18s get in free. Bring your own blankets, chairs, snacks, and beach balls, or enjoy activities and refreshments provided by local businesses, including free beer while it lasts. With four to six shows a year, each one showcasing multiple acts and typically going down outdoors, you get quality time with your kid(s) in the sun, set to the sound of Memphis music. Any and all head-banging welcome.

memphisrocknromp.com

RUN WILD IN THIS BACKYARD

MY BIG BACKYARD AT MEMPHIS BOTANIC GARDEN

I could list several grown-up reasons for you to visit Memphis Botanic Garden: wine tastings, workshops, concerts . . . You should do those. But with kids, you should do one thing: Go wild in My Big Backyard, a progressive playground where young'uns pinball around 13 different vignettes across 2.5 acres. They'll squeal over rushing through a rainbow of playhouses, tunneling through wormholes, dancing in the (automated) rain, hula-hooping on the lawn, climbing into a kid-sized birdhouse and constructing log forts; you'll squeal over tiring them out. Admission to My Big Backyard is included with Memphis Botanic Garden admission.

Though outside of My Big Backyard, two other Memphis Botanic Garden landscapes are natural kid-pleasers: Buy food at the reception desk to feed koi in the Japanese Garden; lead future paleontologists to the Prehistoric Garden, where they can uncover fossils in a sandy dig pit surrounded by ferns and magnolias.

750 Cherry Rd., 901-636-4100, memphisbotanicgarden.com

LINE UP
FOR MAMA D'S ITALIAN ICE

You know those first signs of spring you get all giddy about each year? Chief on my giddy list is the return of the farmers' market to Memphis Botanic Garden (end of April through the end of October, Wednesday, 2–6 p.m.). Yes, temps can get warm, but steal my on-the-spot remedy: With garden admission, spritz yourself at Raindrop Stop, that automated rain shower I mentioned on the previous page. Then skip over to the market—admission is free—and locate Mama D. She'll be the one with the steady string of kid-customers queued up for her scoops of Italian ice and all-natural popsicles. Know something, though? The parents can't resist, so line up with them and order yourself a Hibiscus Mint or Chocolate Sea Salt pop, or anything Mama D's made that week using produce from her fellow vendors. She opened a store in 2014, but promise me you'll meet her this way first.

Mama D's Italian Ice, 305 New Byhalia Rd., #101,
Collierville, 901-221-8126, mymamads.com

PLAY ARCHAEOLOGIST
AT CHUCALISSA

If you grew up in Memphis, chances are, you haven't visited the C.H. Nash Museum/Chucalissa Archaeological Site since you were a school kid. Change that. Before Elvis—heck, before Hernando De Soto—American Indians settled this area. We know this, in part, because Civilian Conservation Corps laborers digging a pool for T.O. Fuller State Park in the 1930s unearthed their village, a mound complex that peaked around 1500 A.D. Today, Chucalissa presents the mounds and Saturday morning programming: During Family Days, follow the half-mile nature trail through an arboretum to the medicinal plant sanctuary, points within T.O. Fuller State Park, and a platform overlooking the bluffs and Mississippi River floodplain (spy for surprises like the Walden-esque writing desk tucked in the woods). On Volunteer Saturdays, drop in to help garden or process artifacts; children are always welcome and assigned creative projects if they require an alternative activity.

C.H. Nash Museum/Chucalissa Archaeological Site, 1987 Indian Village Dr., 901-785-3160, memphis.edu/chucalissa *Closed Monday*

T.O. Fuller State Park, 1500 Mitchell Rd., 901-543-7581, tnstateparks.com/parks/about/t-o-fuller

LEARN FREE
THE PINK PALACE AND LICHTERMAN NATURE CENTER

The Pink Palace is what field trips are made of: taxidermy and skeletons, dinosaur models, vignettes depicting yesteryear Memphis. Traveling exhibits and upgrades keep it fresh—in 2014, the museum's IMAX theater went 3D digital and its planetarium was slated for an update—but it's the oldies that get me. Marvel at the miniature circus and jaunt through the replica Piggly Wiggly: The first self-service grocery was founded by Clarence Saunders and the Pink Palace was (sort of) his home. See the free part on the next page.

The Pink Palace Museum, 3050 Central Ave.,
901-636-2362, memphismuseums.org

Lichterman Nature Center, 5992 Quince Rd., 901-767-7322,
memphismuseums.org/lichterman-overview *Closed Sunday and Monday*

Year-round on Tuesdays, 1 p.m. to close, admission is free to the Pink Palace and Lichterman Nature Center, the museum's East Memphis outpost for easy trail hikes amid forests, lakes, and meadows, plus live animal displays in the Backyard Nature Center.

The Pink Palace and Lichterman also offer **free summer membership**. Look for details on the museum website around May.

Or, **become a member**. Because it's not just about the money you'll save when you make repeat visits to the Pink Palace and Lichterman; it's about the money you'll save when you want to visit any affiliate of the Association of Science–Technology Centers (astc.org). I haven't calculated our savings, but I can tell you how awesome it feels getting in free, or discounted, to pretty much any discovery, nature, or science attraction we've wanted to visit outside of Memphis.

BRING YOUR BOARD WITH YOU
TOBEY SKATE PARK

If you need a glossary to decode what you're about to read, Tobey Park probably isn't for you. Then again, maybe it is, particularly if you're traveling with a skateboarder who needs a fix away from home. The park materialized in 2011 with banks, bowls, half-pipes, ledges, rails, and a snake run. Sound daunting? Don't stress: The features work for advanced to beginner skaters; periodic clinics help, too. Want the inside track? Founder Aaron Shafer recommends showing up on a Saturday morning between 9 and 11 a.m., when he or another member of the crew who advised the design is likely to be around. Ask for a walk-through; then grind while the majority of skaters are still sleeping. Helmets and protective pads are required for ages 12 and under.

2599 Avery Ave., 901-636-6564, skatelifememphis.org

QUIZ YOUR CREW
AT THE COTTON MUSEUM

I frequently direct families to the Cotton Museum, and here's why: You start on the floor of the Memphis Cotton Exchange, active in this building from 1922 to the early 1980s. The room is decked as it appeared in 1939, with oral histories, artifacts, and exhibits added. Next, cross to the Exploration Hall, a collection of vibrant, interactive exhibits: Guess how many pairs of jeans one bale of cotton yields; drench denim with "rain" to see what engineered fiber can do; learn about the dreaded boll weevil in a light-up display; examine a replica gene gun; pick up a cotton sack. Feeling proficient? Challenge your crew to the Hall's cotton trivia game: Spin the wheel on the wall, answer questions, and move a tractor marker to keep score. Winner gets dessert downtown—I call A. Schwab, page 98.

65 Union Ave., 901-531-7826, memphiscottonmuseum.org

COVER 954 MILES IN FIVE BLOCKS
MUD ISLAND RIVER PARK

The address below leads to a paid parking lot where you can board a monorail for an island in the middle of the Mississippi River. The island holds Mud Island River Park, where the Mud Island River Museum introduces you to native tribes, steamboat-era characters, and Delta musicians forever swept in the river's flow—via artifacts and replica vessels like the *Belle of the Bluffs*, a recreated paddle steamer you can board. The roundtrip monorail ride costs $4, or you can buy a package that adds access to the museum. But wading through the island's Riverwalk, a geography lesson disguised as a splash park, is free, and my family's favorite island to-do. Let the little ones slosh about as you linger over the stories of each city detailed by this scale replica (30": 1 mile) that condenses the 954-mile flow of the Lower Mississippi River into five blocks. When you reach the Gulf of Mexico, represented by a million-gallon pool, rent a pedal boat or savor for free the wide-open view of downtown Memphis.

125 N. Front St., 901-576-7241, mudisland.com
Open April through October, Tuesday through Sunday

RIDE THE RIVER
MEMPHIS RIVERBOATS

Memphis Riverboats's *Island Queen* sternwheeler isn't mechanically faithful to her 19th-century prototypes, but she looks the part. Anyway, you'll soon be glued to the Mississippi River panoramas from her open upper decks. March through November, buy tickets and board from Beale Street Landing; daily sightseeing cruises run four miles down the Tennessee side of the river and back up the Arkansas side for a 90-minute roundtrip. Chances are, James Gilmer will be your captain, tour guide, and chief mingler. His script covers Tom Lee to towboats, but don't leave without meeting him personally: It's Gilmer's stories of running the river during the 2011 floods and of being among the first African-American riverboat captains that are truly epic.

In season, Friday and Saturday night dinner cruises—I'm talking live band, full bar—are available, too.

251 Riverside Dr., 901-527-2628, memphisriverboats.net

HAIL THE
AMERICAN QUEEN

The *American Queen* cruised her inaugural season in 2012 from her homeport in Memphis. She's designed to capture the romance of the river with throwback décor, an onboard "riverlorian," and genteel, multiday itineraries along the Mississippi. You might not have the vacation days or dollars to cruise with her, but I bet you've got a few hours on a weekend to tip your hat to her while she's docked. Saturdays, 2–5 p.m., April through June, and again in October and November, are prime time: Stop by Beale Street Landing, watch as passengers return from their land excursions, and listen as the Steamboat Syncopators, the paddle wheeler's six-piece "house" band, welcome them back. Check the cruise schedule before you go to confirm docking location and dates.

251 Riverside Dr., 901-654-2600, americanqueensteamboatcompany.com

IN THE NEIGHBORHOOD:
BAG FOODIE SOUVENIRS AND A MEAL AT MISS CORDELIA'S

I'm not dissuading you from buying the Elvis sunglasses. I'm just saying that food can make a tasty, authentic souvenir, and Miss Cordelia's Grocery, located in the downtown spin-off of Harbor Town (a.k.a. Mud Island), makes a one-stop shop. Choose from 30-plus local and regional products including Pistache French Pastry macarons, handmade in downtown Memphis by Erica Thewis, and Robert Hodum's honey, cultivated in neighboring Collierville. Bonus: The grocery's deli, Cordelia's Table, serves breakfast, lunch, and dinner daily. Command a sandwich, and a table on the patio. Not in the mood to create your own? Order Tom's Poppin' BLT, made with Tom's Tiny Kitchen pimento cheese—you guessed it—made locally. For a proper ending, add on a slice of the caramel or strawberry cake imported from Sugaree's Bakery in Mississippi.

737 Harbor Bend Rd., 901-526-4772, misscordelias.com

... THEN, WALK IT OFF
MISSISSIPPI RIVER GREENBELT PARK

When you turned into the residential side of Harbor Town/
Mud Island to reach Miss Cordelia's Grocery, you had to notice
that swath of green opposite you. Yep, the one fronting the
Mississippi River and anchored by the mammoth trees. That's
Mississippi River Greenbelt Park. If you want an elevated
view, and you don't mind negotiating runner/stroller/dog-
walker traffic, stick to the sidewalk. For a river-level view,
mosey along the generous green. I don't know about you, but
I could journey forever, or at least the three-mile roundtrip,
beneath that leafy canopy. Free parking lots edge the green
space and the northernmost lot maintains a boat ramp. When
river levels are low, you might even find the *American Queen*
docked there.

Mississippi River Greenbelt Park is located along Island Drive
between the A.W. Willis Avenue Bridge and North Mud Island Road

CLAIM THE BEST VIEW OF THE RIVER
THE METAL MUSEUM

Rooftops and riverboats make pretty perches for ogling the Mississippi. But to my eye, the Metal Museum unfurls it best: near a bend in the river that creates angles unlike the head-on vista you get just north in downtown; shrouded by mystic trees, a sculpture garden, and architecture with a story. Go for any museum event—October's annual Repair Days are popular, but most weekends at 2:30 and 3 p.m., you can witness forging and casting demos that remind you: This is a working museum alive with an artist-in-residence and apprentices (and, ahem, it's the only institution in the U.S. devoted to metal art and craft). Before or after the demos, view changing exhibits in the galleries and browse the gift shop, expanding in 2014.

374 Metal Museum Dr., 901-774-6380, metalmuseum.org
Closed Monday

...NEXT TO THIS ONE
JIMMY OGLE TOURS

Jimmy Ogle knows so much Memphis history, you practically have to run to keep up with him and his train of thought on his free city tours. About five times a year (select spring and fall Sundays at 2 p.m.), he slows things down to explore rarely charted territory: the sidewalk along the Memphis & Arkansas Bridge—the only legal sidewalk across the Mississippi River within 500 miles. Ogle's bridge walks begin in Crump Park with a 20-minute orientation to the river and its bluffs, bridges, and barges before making the march. Go at your own pace and as far as you like along the one-mile stretch suspended 100 feet above the river, and see how many questions you can ask Ogle along the way.

jimmyogle.com

TAKE A CUSTOM TOUR
OF ST. BLUES GUITAR WORKSHOP

Like its boutique approach to production, a tour of St. Blues Guitar Workshop is custom. Monday through Saturday at 11 a.m. and 2 p.m., or other times by appointment, an exec or tech will show you the front and back of the operation. The tours run $4 and last about 45 minutes depending on your interests. Don't be afraid to ask anything, whether to try a hand at fretting or playing one of the instruments. Allow extra time to hang at the "Whammy Bar" where Greg Mitchell crafts cigar box guitars, and to meet Tom "TK" Keckler, the father of the Bluesmaster who spends most afternoons checking instrument quality and relating his encounters with Jeff Beck and Led Zeppelin.

645 Marshall Ave., 901-578-3588,
saintblues.com *Closed Sunday, except by appointment*

THEN, TAKE THE ONLY GIBSON TOUR IN THE WORLD
GIBSON BEALE STREET SHOWCASE

Everybody knows the name of this manufacturer that dates to 1902 and produces acoustic and electric guitars, mandolins, and banjos in facilities across the world. But only the Memphis factory allows tours (available for visitors ages 5 and up on the hour Monday through Saturday, 11 a.m.–4 p.m.; Sunday, noon–4 p.m.; $10). For 45 minutes, you'll move from station to station hearing, sometimes seeing, each phase of the production process, a mix of machine and handwork that culminates in persnickety final touches: painting and testing Gibson's ES line of guitars.

Make a reservation. Even with the sizeable groups Gibson accommodates, tours fill up fast. While you're reserving, ask whether luthiers will be working during your tour; particularly on weekends and around holidays, they may not be. You'll especially like this tour if spotting a guitar-in-progress for Dave Grohl or someone like him star-strikes you, or if you're a guitarist—play a demo instrument in the retail center before or after your tour.

145 Lt. George W. Lee Ave., 901-544-7998, gibson.com

SIGHTSEE FOUR WAYS
GUIDED TOURS OF THE BLUFF CITY

If you're considering booking a sightseeing tour, these operators spin 'em four totally different ways.

Backbeat Tours

Backbeat guides tours of all sorts—ghost walks, history talks, etc.—but the 90-minute Mojo Tour's the marquee with drive-bys of legendary-but-lost recording studios and the first Memphis homes of Johnny Cash, B.B. King, and Elvis Presley. P.S.: Your tour guide's a local musician who'll talk, and sing, you through the sights. Participation via onboard tambourines and shakers is voluntary. **Listen up, locals:** You'll probably learn something, and have fun, on the Mojo Tour. But keep an eye on Backbeat's new Memphis Loves Memphis series, a monthly offering of specialty tours from bring-your-dog days to dive-bar crawls. All Backbeat Tours, save the bar crawls, are suitable for all ages.

140 Beale St., 901-272-2328, backbeattours.com

Carriage Company of Memphis

These horse-drawn carriages congregate downtown outside The Peabody (149 Union Ave.) and where Beale Street meets South Second and South Third Streets. You can also call for pick-up almost anywhere downtown. Choose a 30-, 45- or 60-minute ride to take in Beale Street, the riverfront, Court Square, and districts from South Main to The Pinch.

901-507-2587, carriagecomemphis.com

Memphis Hop

Tuesday through Sunday, the Memphis Hop shuttle loops 11 attractions citywide, Graceland, Stax Museum of American Soul Music, and Memphis Zoo among them. Hop on and off as you wish, or hang on for the whole loop. Buy tickets online, onboard, or at select Hop stops. Note that attraction admission is not included, and shuttle frequency lessens October through March. Bonus: Children ages 12 and under ride free, and second-day discounts are available.

901-577-5467, memphishop.com

Segway of Memphis Tours

You need to be 14 for this one, and of course, part of the allure is the mode of transport (relax—your tour begins with 30 minutes of training). For the next 90 minutes, you'll zip past the best of downtown Memphis, and all the juicy bits between. An Elvis-themed tour debuts in 2014.

149 Union Ave., 615-244-0555, segwayofmemphistours.com

LIVE THE DREAM
TAD PIERSON'S AMERICAN DREAM SAFARI

Tad Pierson wants you to see, hear, smell, and rub elbows with Memphis. So, he'll take you on a daytime drive of the city mapped by your interests—that's his Greatest Hits Tour. Just tell him what you're into and he'll chauffeur you around, windows down, for three hours, pointing out the stuff you want to see. I'd ask for a drive by Willie Mitchell's Royal Studios, where the late Mitchell's son, Boo, still produces music. But that's just me.

One more thing: Pierson will be picking you up in his hunk of a car, a 1955 Cadillac sized right for you and a few friends.

If it's Sunday morning, Pierson will take you to Al Green's Full Gospel Tabernacle. But if you want to experience Memphis's living, breathing blues, let him take you on a Juke Joint Tour to neighborhood digs like The Blue Worm. Pierson reports that Sunday nights have been consistently good.

Tad Pierson's American Dream Safari, 901-527-8870

TOUR STAX
WITH A MEMPHIS HORN

Stax Records: You know the hits, but do you know the story? And if you know the story, do you know it like this? Select your level of familiarity on the next page and act accordingly.

Stax Museum of American Soul Music, 926 E. McLemore Ave., 901-942-7685, staxmuseum.com *Closed Monday*

Wayne Jackson Tours, 901-302-8911, waynejacksonmusic.com

"Whatstax?"

That's a play on *Wattstax*—look it up. Though if you're honestly wondering "What's Stax?" your first order should be visiting the Stax Museum of American Soul Music. Located on the site where Stax Records rocked before it was razed, museum exhibits (audio and video) chronicle the studio's heart-tugging, whip-lashing highs and lows, from black-and-white cooperation in an unlikely era to Otis Redding gone-too-soon and Stax's forced bankruptcy.

"Hold on, I'm comin' (around) . . ."

The film you'll see at the top of your museum visit shares the Stax story via interviews with former artists. For a live Q&A, commission Wayne Jackson, sole surviving member of the Memphis Horns, as your museum escort. You can even add on happy hour at Jackson's condo, decorated with 27 Gold Records and his Grammy Lifetime Achievement Award.

"I dig it . . . just let me dance!"

See you on the *Soul Train* dance floor. (Honestly, I usually start dancing in the museum parking lot, where speakers broadcast the hits before drawing me inside to the aforementioned dance floor and Isaac Hayes's rotating, gold-plated Cadillac.)

Bonus:

Watch for the "Entering Soulsville" murals beneath the railroad trestles along South Bellevue Boulevard as you near the museum.

CRANK THE MEMPHIS SOUND
STAX MUSIC ACADEMY AND THE BO-KEYS

Adjacent to the Stax Museum, the extracurricular Stax Music Academy trains students in the soul tradition. The kids can groove. Catch them at Stax to the Max, the free street festival/ feast of live performances that surrounds the museum every late-April, or on Tuesday afternoons throughout June and July, when the Stax Music Academy Alumni Band performs inside the museum's Studio A.

For a veteran intonation of the Memphis sound, follow The Bo-Keys. The roster reads like a who's who of session musicians, mixing Stax and Hi Records alums—Ben Cauley, Howard Grimes, Archie Turner—with younger chops, including Al Gamble and Joe Restivo of The City Champs, page 111, and Scott Bomar, who scored *Hustle & Flow*. In other words, if the percussive horns, funky keys, driving drums, and bass sound familiar, it's partly because you're hearing musicians who've backed Al Green, Isaac Hayes, Rufus and Carla Thomas, and so many others, now with Percy Wiggins and his voluminous voice on lead.

Stax Music Academy, staxmusicacademy.org

The Bo-Keys, thebokeys.com

IN THE NEIGHBORHOOD:
EAT YOUR MEAT-AND-THREE
AT THE FOUR WAY

If you don't know, the "and three" equals cornbread plus two sides. And though the meat-and-three is a Southern/soul menu convention, you *must* eat it at The Four Way. Not only because the restaurant has helped anchor Memphis's Soulsville neighborhood since 1946, or because it's where Martin Luther King Jr. ate when he was in town. Eat here because owner Willie Earl Bates, and his English peas, are so sweet, you won't need dessert. I usually order mine with country-fried steak and turnip greens; my friend Tim swears by the turkey and dressing, but sometimes curses about a diet and orders the baked fish. Whether you're counting comfort or calories, you won't leave wanting.

998 Mississippi Blvd., 901-507-1519,
fourwaymemphis.com *Closed Monday*

REPEAT:
ELMWOOD CEMETERY IS A PARK.

True, Elmwood is a cemetery. But it was established in 1852 as a park, with bandstands and a trolley delivering citizens to its gate. "They came to visit their ancestors, but also to socialize in the fresh air," reminds Kimberly McCollum, Elmwood's executive director. (If you were waiting for one, consider *that* your invitation.) With a little planning, get in on year-round events from lunchtime lectures to October's Twilight Tour guided by costumed interpreters. Personally, I take my Elmwood hushed: Park along any curb—roads wind throughout the park—and set out with your camera and/or running shoes and/or dog and/or nothing at all; you've got 80 acres and 160-plus years of history, as told by fairytale trees and romantic statuary, to cover. For an instant itinerary, loop the cemetery's mile-long perimeter or call on the cottage at the entrance for the $10 audio tour or $2 tree map (Elmwood is a Level 2 arboretum).

824 S. Dudley St., 901-774-3212,
elmwoodcemetery.org *Cottage closed Sunday*

WHILE YOU'RE AT ELMWOOD...
ELMWOOD CEMETERY VAULT, LIBRARY, AND PROGRAMS

Are you inside the cottage at Elmwood's entrance? Good. Look to your left. That's the vault, added in 1904; now the gift shop. Note the city directories on its shelves, dating to 1859, each one thick as a brick. Now, cross the lobby to the historian's office. It's a parlor room where you're welcome to ask questions and use the slight-but-mighty library, stacked with first editions and out-of-prints. It's okay to fixate on the furniture, too: That green sofa originated in 18th-century France before coming to Memphis and the Crump family—more on them in the cemetery should you need an introduction.

If you're really into reading and history, Elmwood's bi-monthly "Read in Peace" book club has your name written all over it. Meeting dates and book selections are published well in advance, so even out-of-towners can participate. Just call ahead for a reservation; no fee.

824 S. Dudley St., 901-774-3212,
elmwoodcemetery.org *Cottage closed Sunday*

SHRINE ON
CRYSTAL SHRINE GROTTO AT MEMORIAL PARK CEMETERY

Scene: 1930s Memphis. E.C. Hinds visualizes a different kind of cemetery for the city: one where nature, and art inspired by it, prevail over high-rise grave markers. Enter Mexican artist Dionicio Rodriguez and his peculiar talent for sculpting and coloring concrete. Access Memorial Park Cemetery today from Poplar Avenue and you'll come to Rodriguez's Fountain of Youth and Wishing Chair first, modest preludes to his Crystal Shrine Grotto. For a preview, imagine a geode swallowed you: Sparkly stalactites and wall formations surround. Biblical vignettes set within present statuary backed by mosaics and metallic murals. Outside the Grotto, trace garden paths and sculpted foot bridges, rest on a carved bench to watch fish swim in the Pool of Hebron, peer into the castle-y Cave of Machpelah and stand inside Abraham's Oak, an immersive example of Rodriguez's faux-bois technique.

One more thing: You can find Isaac Hayes's grave directly across from the Pool of Hebron.

5668 Poplar Ave., 901-767-8930, memorialparkfuneralandcemetery.com

MEET THE VENUS OF MEMPHIS
DIXON GALLERY & GARDENS

I understand if you don't know her. On several visits to the Dixon Gallery & Gardens, I haven't made it past the cutting garden, and if I have, it's commonly because I'm dying to see what's on display from the permanent collection or traveling exhibits. If you have to, dedicate one visit to drift elsewhere: Across the 17-acre grounds, you'll discover garden rooms just as the late Hugo Dixon planned them, receive a shady reminder of the Dixon's arboretum status, and come upon allées and statuary, including the Italian marble *Venus of Memphis* commissioned by the Dixons in 1963. Bonus: Tuesdays, 10 a.m.–4 p.m., pay what you can to enter the gallery and gardens. Saturday admission, 10 a.m.–noon, is free, including Family Studio art-making activities (first Saturdays monthly, 10:30 a.m.–12:30 p.m.).

4339 Park Ave., 901-761-5250, dixon.org *Closed Monday*

IN THE NEIGHBORHOOD:
EAT IN SOMEONE'S HOME
(Hudman/Ticer Edition)
ANDREW MICHAEL ITALIAN KITCHEN AND
HOG + HOMINY/THE HOLDING PEN

Brookhaven Circle in East Memphis is a residential cove repurposed as a commercial cluster that includes the mounting culinary empire of Michael Hudman and Andrew Ticer. Play multiple choice with the options on the next page ("all" is an acceptable answer).

Andrew Michael Italian Kitchen, 712 W. Brookhaven Cir.,
901-347-3569, andrewmichaelitaliankitchen.com
Closed Sunday and Monday except No-Menu
Mondays (final Mondays monthly)

Hog + Hominy/The Holding Pen, 707 W. Brookhaven Cir.,
901-207-7396, hogandhominy.com

Reserve a table at **Andrew Michael Italian Kitchen**. Cocktails here are impeccably executed, and plans to augment the bar in 2014 will make it easier to order another round. Eventually, you'll get hungry. Make sure you've reserved a table in advance—the back deck underscores the eating-in-someone's-home thing, particularly when you notice the herb garden.

Hit Andrew Michael Italian Kitchen on **No-Menu Monday**, a prix-fixe, four-course dinner the chefs use as a means of introducing less-familiar tastes to diners. Hudman and Ticer recommend reserving three weeks ahead.

Lunch, dinner, or late-night, go sans-reservation to **Hog + Hominy**, where the chefs' Italian family recipes and Southern-American roots get all comfy-cozy. If you hear records spinning out back, push through the bookcase (between the kitchen and the bathroom) to unlock **The Holding Pen**. When it's "rockin'," as the chefs say, you'll find a bartender and surprises on this patio—say Frito pie in the crockpot.

MAKE YOURSELF AT HOME
IN CENTRAL GARDENS

You're driving west along Central Avenue when the houses hulk. Your vision goes all front porches and porte-cochères and arbors. You want to slow down; study the homes; peek behind their parapets. Do it Sunday afternoon following Labor Day during the Central Gardens Association Home & Garden Tour. This National Historic District and Level 3 arboretum is truly a mix of homes grand and petite, old and new-made-to-look-old . . . a popped-up encyclopedia of early 20th-century architectural styles. A changing lineup of six to seven private residences annually ensures you'll see a variety, and docents at each home will ensure you know your Queen Annes from your Craftsmen; then coax out family heirlooms. As long as you're venturing onto private property, enjoy a beverage at the University Club, the members-only organization that serves as the tour's hospitality hub. It was built on land owned by Clarence Saunders, founder of Piggly Wiggly and erstwhile Central Gardens resident.

Central Gardens Association Home & Garden Tour,
901-343-6242, centralgardens.org
University Club, 1346 Central Ave., 901-722-3700, ucmem.com

FIND TIFFANY
AT GRACE-ST. LUKE'S

Churches grew amid Central Gardens's historic homes. And like many of those homes, the churches can hold significance outside *and* in. Grace-St. Luke's Episcopal Church preserves seven Tiffany windows you must see from inside to appreciate, including a turn-of-the-20th-century depiction of the ascension that awes over the chapel entrance. Additional fenestrations present annunciation and resurrection angels, the nativity, and Jesus as a boy in the temple and in Joseph's carpentry shop. Weekdays, poke in the church office for a brochure to direct a self-guided look. To enhance the view, consider this: Church records suggest that a benefactor met an associate of Louis Comfort Tiffany's at a Paris Exposition, and that Tiffany himself supervised the original installation of the benefactor's early commissions.

1720 Peabody Ave., 901-272-7425, gracestlukes.org

DON'T TAKE THESE HOMES FOR GRANTED
MAGEVNEY AND MALLORY-NEELY HOMES

You might not realize the momentousness of touring Memphis's historic Magevney and Mallory-Neely homes. They escaped the overworked wrecking ball of urban renewal only to be shuttered for years by budget cuts. Today, their doors are open again to you, so show 'em you prize 'em by paying a visit and listening to their stories. For its part, the 1830s Magevney House is Memphis's oldest residence, diminutive with similarly intimate displays like the family Bible and Mrs. Magevney's wee garden out back. (Open for free tours first Saturdays monthly, 1–4 p.m.) In contrast, the circa-1852 Mallory-Neely House is a study in opulence, a 25-room Italianate Villa flaunting 95 percent of its original décor. Your eyes may need a rest taking in the first-floor double parlor, which includes Antonio Canova's *Psyche Revived by Cupid's Kiss*, a Louvre holding, replicated in solid marble over onyx and supported by a brick pillar in the basement. Open for tours Friday and Saturday, 10 a.m.–3 p.m. on the hour.

Mallory-Neely House, 652 Adams Ave., 901-523-1484,
memphismuseums.org/mallory_neely-overview

Magevney House, 198 Adams Ave., 901-523-1484,
memphismuseums.org/magevney-overview

TIME-TRAVEL IN COLLIERVILLE

Collierville sits 30 minutes southeast of Memphis, but can feel centuries removed considering its ornamental cannons, preserved churches, and postcard of a town square. Start at the Morton Museum of Collierville History, a pocket of exhibits inside circa-1873 Collierville Christian Church. Before you leave, enter the former sanctuary, glorious with stained glass and spindles, and gather two brochures: one that points you to the preserved exteriors of four additional churches within walking distance; the other, Collierville's Civil War Walking Tour, a compact route blazed by interpretive signs detailing the 1863 Battle of Collierville, and how General William Tecumseh Sherman nearly incinerated the town. Listen as you tramp for the rhythmic railing of the train and the random chiming of "Amazing Grace."

Morton Museum of Collierville History, 196 N. Main St., Collierville, 901-457-2650, colliervillemuseum.org *Closed Sunday through Tuesday*

THEN, SQUARE UP
COLLIERVILLE'S TOWN SQUARE

You've trekked past Collierville's historic churches and Civil War sites. You're hungry and wondering what's with the rail cars lined up downtown. Regroup on The Square, a spoil of green space, benches, bike racks, public restrooms, and shops fringed by free parking and those vintage rail cars. The cars are open Monday through Friday, 9 a.m.–4 p.m., for free—don't miss the hat racks and tiny kitchen of the 1940s-era "executive" rail car. Step off toward The Square, where window and sidewalk displays lure you to shop for anything from cowboy boots to jewelry trends, and you can nab lunch and a cup of regionally crafted Sweet Magnolia gelato at Square Beans. Flavors change but they're ever-indulgent, like Sweet Tea Sorbetto and Whiskey and Pecan Gelato. Better yet? Take dessert to go and enjoy it on one of those benches I mentioned.

Main Street Collierville (for additional information on walking tours and The Square), 125 N. Rowlett St., Collierville, 901-853-1666, mainstreetcollierville.org *Closed Saturday and Sunday*

Square Beans, 103 N. Center St., Collierville, 901-854-8855, squarebeans.com *Closed most Sundays*

GET ON BOARD
MEMPHIS RAILROAD & TROLLEY MUSEUM

Imagine an age when 50 railroad arrivals and departures chugged in and out of Memphis daily. Hard to visualize? Not at the Memphis Railroad & Trolley Museum. Located inside circa-1914 Central Station, the museum displays original time tables along with scale replicas, model train set-ups, a Thomas & Friends–themed nook for young enthusiasts, and technology—manual and electronic switches, even rail signals you can push a button to flash. If you like aged spaces as much as I do, ask a staff member to point you to the station's bygone waiting room, now a special events venue where an antique call-board hangs and sunlight streams. Then, ask for a look inside the former baggage and freight tunnel, strewn with century-old baggage carts.

545 S. Main St., #121, 901-590-3099, mrtm.org
Closed Monday through Thursday

THIS TIME, FOR REAL: GET ON BOARD
RIDE THE DOWNTOWN TROLLEYS

Exhibits inside the Memphis Railroad & Trolley Museum expose the origin of trolleys in the city as mule-drawn streetcars around 1866. Step outside the museum to see and ride their evolution: a fleet of trolleys, charmingly restored so that solid brass and mahogany accents shine (the glue-chip transom windows are a sight, too). Travel three lines: Main Street, which connects districts from The Pinch to South Main; Riverfront, a thorough loop that compounds the Main Street line with a stretch along the Mississippi; and Madison, serving the medical district. Look for stations throughout downtown and Midtown, and bring exact change for the fare box: Base fare is $1 one way, and no change is given or made on board. Daily and monthly passes are available; see website for details.

matatransit.com/services/trolleys *No Madison Line service on Sunday*

IN THE NEIGHBORHOOD:
ORDER BREAKFAST AT LUNCH—
THE ARCADE RESTAURANT AND BON TON CAFÉ

When you rock-and-roll all night, you need breakfast any time of day, or at least until mid-afternoon, when Bon Ton Café and The Arcade stop serving it. Both restaurants are long-timers downtown—Bon Ton dating to 1945; The Arcade to 1919— with the apt newspaper clippings hung about, though The Arcade one-ups the recently remodeled Bon Ton with its greasy-spoon patina and movie connections (read the historic marker for the highlights).

Back to breakfast: I declare Bon Ton's buttermilk biscuits smothered in sausage gravy the best in town, distinguished, and made even more stick-to-you, by green and red peppers. The Arcade's made-your-way omelets nod to the diner's Greek heritage with mix-ins like artichoke, roasted garlic, and feta, if you can resist daily lunch specials like country-fried steak.

Bon Ton Café, 150 Monroe Ave., 901-525-0883,
bontoncafememphis.com

The Arcade Restaurant, 540 S. Main St., 901-526-5757,
arcaderestaurant.com

REFLECT ON
THE NEW NATIONAL CIVIL RIGHTS MUSEUM

Now's a better time than ever to visit the National Civil Rights Museum, considering the $28 million overhaul it unveiled in 2014.

What's the same? The Lorraine Motel portion of the museum retains the Montgomery and Freedom Rides buses, Edmond Pettus Bridge, Sit-In Counter, Memphis Sanitation Truck, and viewing of Martin Luther King Jr.'s room (as well as the adjacent room). The museum's Legacy Building annex, located in the boarding house where James Earl Ray allegedly fired the shot that killed King, remains unchanged: Tour it to consider extensive evidence associated with the manhunt, investigation, and indictment following King's murder, and the chilling line-of-sight from the boarding house to King's Lorraine Motel room across the street.

What's new? Outdoor listening posts featuring personal stories related to Memphis's 1968 sanitation strike, King's assassination and the Lorraine Motel. A touch screen mapping school desegregation. More than 40 new films and oral histories throughout, from Freedom Riders to March on Washington participants. An enlarged cell you can enter to hear King reading his "Letter from Birmingham Jail." A Smart Table that invites you to weigh contemporary civil rights topics. And a Mountaintop Theatre where you can view footage of King's final speech.

450 Mulberry St., 901-521-9699, civilrightsmuseum.org *Closed Tuesday*

MAP MLK IN MEMPHIS
MASON TEMPLE, THE FOUR WAY, AND OTHER MLK-CONNECTED SITES

If you've toured the National Civil Rights Museum, you've stood where Martin Luther King Jr.'s time ended in Memphis. Trace his steps back on a driving tour. Mason Temple (930 Mason St.), today the international sanctuary and headquarters of the Church of God in Christ, gave the pulpit to King and his "Mountaintop" speech on the eve of his assassination. Next, navigate to the East Memphis corner of Colonial Road and Sea Isle Road, where a historic marker installed in 2014 remembers sanitation workers Echol Cole and Robert Walker, killed nearby on the job in February 1968. Their deaths sparked the Sanitation Workers' Strike that brought King to Memphis. Round out your MLK itinerary with lunch or dinner at The Four Way, page 47, and a visit to The Withers Collection Museum & Gallery, page 67.

(ART) WALK
SOUTH MAIN HISTORIC DISTRICT

South Main Street is that bridge between the historic and the hip; Trolley Night is its street party. Experience it the final Friday of every month, 6–9 p.m., when resident shops, galleries, restaurants, and bars open their doors wide, pour drinks, and host surprises from art showings to music, dance, and theatrical performances. Bonus: Hop on the trolley anytime during the event—it's free, and in nice weather, you might find musicians performing on board. On and beyond Trolley Night, my South Main staples are:

477store in Memphis College of Art's Nesin Graduate Center, where you can take home work by students, faculty/staff, and alumni. 477 S. Main St., 901-272-5198, 477store.com

Sachë, where it won't surprise you to learn that the bold men's tees and hand-sewn women's shirts and dresses are created by an art-schooler-turned-graffiti artist. Said designer, Eric Evans, carries body products and accessories for men and women, too. 525 S. Main St., 901-922-5549, sachedesign.com

D'Edge Art and Unique Treasures, next page

gosouthmain.com/trolley-night

VIEW ART ON THE EDGE
D'EDGE ART AND UNIQUE TREASURES

Since 2001, artist Debra Edge has operated D'Edge Art and Unique Treasures on South Main Street. The buzz of Trolley Night becomes the color-saturated, folky hubbub; Friday through Sunday afternoons paint a more subdued picture—in warmer months, you might even find George Hunt at work in the studio downstairs. Hunt's work has hung from the Rock and Roll Hall of Fame and Museum to the White House; inside D'Edge, it's his blues musicians and rural characters that dominate. But don't overlook Heather Prouty's pottery, NJ Woods's fanciful rustics, or Alex Warble's paintings (you'll know them when you see robots, cats, loaves of white bread, and Elvis in the same composition). Bonus: D'Edge balances oversized canvases and weighty mixed-media pieces with magnets and gift cards. Cash-and-carry keepsakes: check.

550 S. Main, 901-521-0054, dedgeart.com
Closed Monday through Thursday

STUMBLE ON THIS CELEB PHOTOGRAPHER
ROBINSON GALLERY

Jack Robinson photographed everyone who was anyone in 1960s fashion and pop culture. He worked for the magazines and newspapers everyone was reading: *Life, Vogue, The New York Times.* Yet, he lived the latter part of his life quietly in Memphis. So quietly, in fact, the city wasn't wholly clued into his body of work until after his death. Ask a staff member at Robinson Gallery to relate the story; then survey the photographer's black-and-white celebrity portraits and neon-charged streetscapes on two levels of exhibit space.

Souvenir potential: Buy the gallery's coffee table book of Robinson's work ($40) and the staff will include an 8x8 print—your choice of Joni Mitchell, Jack Nicholson, The Who, or Tina Turner (she's from West Tennessee, you know).

400 S. Front St., 901-576-0708, robinsongallery.com
Closed Saturday and Sunday, except by appointment

LOOK THROUGH ERNEST WITHERS'S LENS

THE WITHERS COLLECTION MUSEUM & GALLERY

Among individual photographers covering the U.S. civil rights movement, Ernest Withers is commonly credited with producing the vastest body of work. Before his death, Withers told his daughter Rosalind that his portfolio was five million images strong. She stopped counting a few years back at one million. The highlights hang inside The Withers Collection Museum & Gallery, a Beale Street storefront that housed Withers's studio. There is happiness here: Negro League Baseball portraits; two would-be kings (B.B. and Elvis) smiling. And there is a heaviness: bus boycotts, protests, and school desegregation documented; graphic stills taken moments after the murders of Emmett Till and Martin Luther King Jr. You may need an hour to see the collection, and many more to process what you've seen.

333 Beale St., 901-523-2344, thewitherscollection.com
Closed Monday and Tuesday

GET A LOAD OF THIS BROAD
BROAD AVENUE ARTS DISTRICT

This broad is Broad Avenue. She's an original. Get to know her on a weekday when her loading docks are loading docks—on weekends, one becomes Water Tower Pavilion, an amphitheater where you might watch others dance or cut in yourself. And so it goes on Broad, a mash-up of industry and creativity that'll keep you coming back for reasons like those on the next page.

The Broad Avenue Arts District is loosely defined by
North Hollywood Street, Broad Avenue, Collins Street,
and Sam Cooper Boulevard, broadavearts.com

Five in One Social Club, 2535 Broad Ave., fiveinone.org *Hours vary*

The Cove, 2559 Broad Ave., 901-730-0719, thecovememphis.com

Three Angels Diner, 2617 Broad Ave., 901-452-1111,
threeangelsdiner.com *Closed Monday*

Water Tower Pavilion, 2542 Broad Ave.

Twice-annual **art walks** (in spring and fall): Follow the Broad Avenue Arts District website or social pages for these and other events.

Photo ops: French street artist Guillaume "Remed" Alby cloaked a Broad Avenue warehouse in mural, but color and grunge coexist everywhere you look in the district. Bring your camera.

Five in One Social Club offers pay-as-you-go art-making sessions and striking souvenirs from 18 local artists, covering posters, tees, and kids' stuff.

Drinks and eats: You know about **Wiseacre**, page 15. Disappear into **The Cove** for cocktails, oysters, and nightly goings-on. With kids, hit **Three Angels Diner** for the changing veggie plate and lemon icebox pie.

The promise of what's to come: The debut of **Water Tower Pavilion** in 2014 added another trinket to Broad's funky charm bracelet. Through 2015, watch as the **Hampline**, page 84, and additional public art adorn the district.

SMILE FOR AMURICA
JAMIE HARMON'S AMURICA PHOTO BOOTH AND STUDIO

If there's one souvenir photo you need of Memphis, it's a portrait inside the Amurica photo booth. Freelance photographer Jamie Harmon fashioned the original booth in 2011 by bedazzling the interior of a 1959 silver teardrop trailer with string lights and choose-your-own props: wigs, sunglasses, masks, baby dolls, a plastic goat. . . . Since then, he's opened a studio and added two photo booth trailers—one mobile, one stationary, both exquisitely out-there. When the booths aren't rented for private events, Harmon and friends pull them around town and host periodic in-studio events, when you can sit for a portrait or pile in the photo booth with pals and take home a print for a fee, usually $10–$30. Follow @amuricaphoto for details.

410 N. Cleveland St., 901-606-2041, amurica.com

DO COOPER-YOUNG BY DAY
COOPER-YOUNG HISTORIC DISTRICT

Midtown's Cooper-Young neighborhood concentrates retail, bars, and restaurants for those days you want to park and walk wherever your mood takes you. Start at the I Love Memphis mural at South Cooper Street and York Avenue. Continue south on Cooper to your choice of stops—maybe Black Lodge Video, page 73, Memphis Drum Shop, page 74, or Burke's Book Store—skim the collection of Memphis-related and signed titles. Turn east onto Young Avenue to thumb through vinyl at Goner Records, page 107. Back on Cooper, snag locally made mementos at Allie Cat Arts, run by a Memphis College of Art graduate. Then, scout a dinner location.

Black Lodge Video, 831 S. Cooper St., 901-272-7744

Memphis Drum Shop, 878 S. Cooper St., 901-276-2328, memphisdrumshop.com *Closed Sunday*

Burke's Book Store, 936 S. Cooper St., 901-278-7484, burkesbooks.com

Goner Records, 2152 Young Ave., 901-722-0095, goner-records.com

Allie Cat Arts, 961 S. Cooper St., 901-722-0094 *Closed Monday through Wednesday*

...AND NIGHT
COOPER-YOUNG HISTORIC DISTRICT

Should you struggle to decide which restaurant or bar to try in Cooper-Young, try 'em all. Think of the neighborhood as a progressive party: Inquire at Tsunami what Chef Ben Smith's up to—the veteran with a passion for the Pacific Rim changes his small plates nightly. Sit a spell on the patio at Celtic Crossing; depending on the night, the Irish pub/restaurant might deliver trivia, a DJ, or live music. Share a plate and artisan cocktails at Alchemy. Take the late shift at Young Avenue Deli to yell at whatever's on the projection screen or catch a concert; the giant bar and always-available menu will sustain you. Reminder: Cooper-Young is also Karen Carrier territory, page 113.

Tsunami, 928 S. Cooper St., 901-274-2556,
tsunamimemphis.com *Closed Sunday*

Celtic Crossing, 903 S. Cooper St., 901-274-5151,
celticcrossingmemphis.com

Alchemy Memphis, 940 S. Cooper St., 901-726-4444,
alchemymemphis.com

Young Avenue Deli, 2119 Young Ave., 901-278-0034,
youngavenuedeli.com

SUSPEND DISBELIEF
AT BLACK LODGE VIDEO

Bryan Hogue and Matt Martin remember when they were the ones oohing and aahing at other people's video stores. Their Black Lodge Video puts them on the offering end, and they think that's cool, too. So don't feel weird, even if you're not renting a movie, to go in. Show off the collection to a friend. Gape at the number and variety of titles, thousands of them across periods, genres, and directors, on DVD and (gasp) VHS. If the Lodge is open, a movie will be playing. If you like it, let one of the couches or chairs suck you in for a cinematic pit stop. Of course, if you're renting, count on the guys to recommend something that'll make *you* ooh and aah—if that's what you're in the mood for.

831 S. Cooper St., 901-272-7744

FEEL THE VIBRATION
MEMPHIS DRUM SHOP

If nearly every musician coming through Memphis makes a pilgrimage to Memphis Drum Shop (MDS), why shouldn't you? Part retail store, part percussionist's shrine, MDS stocks souvenir sticks, hosts concerts and clinics on a soundstage, and provides an unamplified electronic kit you can demo. For an exclusive, register for Sonic Massage with Faye Henry, usually offered final Saturdays monthly at 1 p.m. ($60 for the hour). Inside MDS's private gong chamber, Henry plays 40 Paiste-brand gongs, sized from seven inches to seven feet in diameter, and arranged in a circle (that seven-footer, by the way, is thought to be the only one of its size in the world). The physical vibration in-the-round can be therapeutic, if not transformative. Contact the shop to register.

878 S. Cooper St., 901-276-2328, memphisdrumshop.com *Closed Sunday*

RUB DANNY'S NOSE FOR GOOD LUCK
ST. JUDE CHILDREN'S RESEARCH HOSPITAL

It's hard to imagine that St. Jude Children's Research Hospital, today with 3,800 employees on 66 acres in Memphis, boosted by outreach efforts in 14 countries, began as a deal founder Danny Thomas struck with the patron saint of lost causes. A free, hour-long tour conveys the organization's history and mission: to treat children with incurable diseases no matter their background or ability to pay. In the Patient Care Center, you'll pass parents pulling patients in red wagons; in the Research Building, you'll learn of St. Jude's total therapy approach (that's also where you'll rub the nose of a sculpted Danny Thomas for good luck). All tours must be scheduled in advance, which is an ideal time to discuss the opportunities on the next page.

St. Jude Children's Research Hospital tours,
332 N. Lauderdale St., 901-578-2042, stjude.org

Will the Pavilion be open during your visit? That's the gold-domed building on campus that highlights Danny Thomas as an entertainer and humanitarian alongside St. Jude milestones. Special events close it from time to time (call 901-595-4414 to find out), but you can always step into the adjacent memorial garden, where Danny and wife Rose Marie are buried. Note that hospital tours are available for visitors ages 16 and up; the Pavilion is open to all ages.

Want to donate blood or platelets while you're onsite? Call ahead to the Blood Donor Center (901-595-2024) for a short pre-screen and to schedule an appointment before or after your tour.

LOG 26.2
(or Scream Like a, Well, Cheerleader)
ST. JUDE MEMPHIS MARATHON WEEKEND

The St. Jude Memphis Marathon Weekend owns the first week-end in December annually. As long as you aren't crowd-averse, it's one of the best times to be in Memphis, when the spirit of the city is riding high on a sea of 20,000 people participating in the weekend's marathon, half-marathon, marathon relay, 5K, kids' marathon, and family fun run, and raising some $8 million in the process. Registration opens in May. Back-up plan: Make posters and gather cowbells Friday night; station yourself early Saturday along the marathon route to cheer. If you've been training, the marathon course reads like a "best of" Memphis as it tracks the Mississippi River, Beale Street, Overton Park, page 87, and the St. Jude campus.

stjudemarathon.org

RUN TO THIS ROOFTOP AFTER-PARTY
GIBSON GUITAR 5K RUN/WALK

Don't feel like going the distance? Me either. Let's be back-of-the-pack buddies at the Gibson Guitar 5K Run/Walk, an evening race held annually in mid-June. From the Beale Street start line, course over cobblestones and flow with the Mississippi along Riverside Drive. You'll be motivated, or at least distracted, by the late sun pastel-painting the sky over the river. Cross the finish line outside the Gibson Beale Street Showcase, page 40, and celebrate with refreshments—of course, beer is a refreshment—on the roof.

gibsonguitar5k.racesonline.com

PADDLE THE WOLF

If the Wolf River you know intersects Mississippi River industry, you're wondering why I'm telling you to do this. It's because I want you to head east, about 50 miles to Moscow, Tennessee, where the Wolf is all cypress trees and grassy islands and forested walls, thanks in part to advocacy efforts by the Wolf River Conservancy. Mid-March through mid-November, Ghost River Outfitters will hook you up with a canoe, kayak, or stand-up paddle board, life vests, and paddles to explore the upper Wolf. Call ahead and Mark Babb and crew will have your gear ready whether you want to rent by the hour (weekends from noon 'til sunset), commission guide service, or run the Ghost, the primordial section of the Wolf that flows through five ecosystems in eight miles. Babb's Ghost River run takes 3–5 hours by kayak ($40); 4–6 hours by canoe ($50) and includes shuttle service and gear.

901-485-1220, ghostriverrentals.com

HANG WITH A RANGER
MEEMAN-SHELBY FOREST STATE PARK

Memorial Day through Labor Day, seasonal interpretive rangers staff Meeman-Shelby Forest State Park. For $1, they'll pontoon you around the park's Poplar Tree Lake and identify anything from coral colonies growing underwater to red-eared sliders sunning on semi-submerged logs to mimosa trees fringing the shoreline to some-200 bird species flying overhead, including herons and Mississippi kites. Rent a canoe at the lake's concession to extend your exploration. Afterward, cool off inside the nature center, where rangers have been known to stage impromptu, hands-on reptile programs. While you're with them, ask the rangers about guided hikes and deep swamp canoe trips.

910 Riddick Rd., 901-876-5215,
tnstateparks.com/parks/about/meeman-shelby

Tip

Visiting outside of interpretive ranger season? Meeman-Shelby Forest State Park is quieter, cooler, and abloom in early spring with snow-white dogwoods, lavender phlox, and stands of sunny wildflowers.

TRUMP CENTRAL PARK
SHELBY FARMS PARK

At 4,500 acres, Memphis's Shelby Farms Park is five times larger than New York City's Central Park. In other words, it *can* be all things to all people, with seasonal canoe, kayak, SUP, bike, and horseback riding concessions to help you forge lakes and trails; a disc golf course and laser tag and paintball outfitters to score points with your crew; a resident herd of buffalo to photograph; and the Woodland Discovery Playground, where kids can shoot out of a tower on a 26-foot slide, crawl across a series of rope "webs" into a tree platform, and lounge in a nest swing. (The park is just as pleasant if you've got nothing but your walking shoes.) Construction is projected from 2014–2016 to make Shelby Farms even better—plans sketch a café and restaurant, an expanded lake and trails—but you'll be able to play around it.

500 North Pine Lake Dr., 901-767-7275, shelbyfarmspark.org

CYCLE THE COUNTRY'S MOST IMPROVED BIKE CITY
BIKE TRAILS, RENTALS, AND PIT STOPS

It wasn't long ago that Memphis was shamed for its unfriendliness toward cyclists. In a speedy turn facilitated by the city and grass-roots groups, the movement got wheels, carving bike lanes and rails-to-trails like the Shelby Farms Greenline, a 6.5-mile green corridor paved safely through the heart of the city to Shelby Farms Park. Amid the improvements, that "most improved" nod came from *Bicycling* magazine. Pick up the Shelby Farms Greenline (shelbyfarmspark.org/shelbyfarmsgreenline) from Shelby Farms Park or any of the points on the next page.

From the Shelby Farms Greenline's west end

. . . at Tillman Street and Walnut Grove Road. Park near Republic Coffee for a pre- or post-ride snack: 2924 Walnut Grove Rd., 901-590-1578, republiccoffeememphis.com

At access points mid-route

In particular, Highland Street, High Point Terrace, Graham Street, Waring Road, and Podesta Street provide street parking within neighborhoods and shorten the route in case you're no endurance racer.

Coming soon:

The Hampline, a connector between the Shelby Farms Greenline's western trailhead and Overton Park, page 87

Need a bike while you're in town?

Ask your hotel, or contact one of these local bike shops for a rental:

Midtown Bike Company, 517 S. Main St., 901-522-9757, midtownbikecompany.com *Closed Sunday*

Peddler Bike Shop Memphis, 575 S. Highland St., 901-327-4833, peddlerbikeshop.com

ROLL UP ON A GRIZZ PARTY
TOUR DE GRIZZ

Tour de Grizz is a group bike ride from the Memphis Zoo, home of grizzly bears, to the FedEx Forum, home of the NBA Memphis Grizzlies, and back. It happens annually in March or April, usually coinciding with the Grizzlies's last regular season home game. Your registration fee includes zoo admission, participation in the ride, a ticket to the evening's Grizzlies game and bike valet at the zoo and the Forum. The 10-mile roundtrip ride is magic: It's you in a parade of spandexed road warriors, parents pulling babies in bike trailers, and kids who've just learned to ride. Memphis Police Department shuts down Union Avenue just for you; then escorts you through neighborhoods and back roads to reach downtown and the party in progress outside FedEx Forum. Listen to the beat of the Grizzlies Drumline in the shadow of Beale Street and anticipate the NBA electricity that awaits inside.

grizzlies.com

ROUND THE BASES WITH ROCKEY
THE MEMPHIS REDBIRDS AND AUTOZONE PARK

AutoZone Park is home to the Memphis Redbirds, Triple-A affiliate of the St. Louis Cardinals. Though it opened in 2000, the ballpark still feels new, maybe because it's clean and handsome, built of brick and back-dropped by the downtown Memphis skyline. Still, you'll find me in the cheap seats—the trim lawn seating beyond left field known as the bluff. Here, my daughter can wiggle all she wants; dribble her ice cream (served in a miniature baseball hat, natch); sprint to the adjacent playground; and play midway-style games on the nearby boardwalk. Bring a blanket and a camera: Following Sunday home games, kids can run the bases and take photos with Rockey, the Redbirds's mascot.

200 Union Ave., 901-721-6000, memphisredbirds.com

COUNT HOW MANY THINGS YOU CAN DO IN THIS PARK
(You're Gonna Need More Than One Day.)
OVERTON PARK

Pretend you're given 342 acres to design a park. What do you equip it with? A zoo? An art museum? An art school? An amphitheater? A golf course? A veterans' memorial? A greensward? An old forest? A playground? Nah—two playgrounds. Since 1902, Overton Park has steadily added them all. Count how many you can cram into a day or three. With kids, be sure to include a stop at Rainbow Lake Playground, where a 2013 redo added a classic merry-go-round and a 30-foot-long rope bridge in the sky (or eight feet off the ground, depending on your imagination). Find more ideas over the next four pages.

Overton Park is bounded by North Parkway, East Parkway,
Poplar Avenue, and McLean Boulevard, overtonpark.org

STUDY THE MEMPHIS MASTERS
MEMPHIS BROOKS MUSEUM OF ART

Traveling exhibitions will vie for your attention at the Memphis Brooks Museum of Art, so focus for me: Take one day to study the Memphis Masters—painter Carroll Cloar and photographers Ernest Withers, page 67, and William Eggleston. The Brooks's permanent collection favors these men who lived and worked in Memphis: Cloar blending Southern realities and fantasies on canvas; Withers documenting the civil rights era in moments; Eggleston turning the everyday into the arresting through his lens. Eye for images by Withers and Eggleston in the lobby, where each photographer commands a wall; discover Cloar throughout the building (start on the first floor by the elevators; then check the Moss Mezzanine). With 184 images by Withers, 279 by Eggleston, and 30 by Cloar in rotation, the Brooks gives you plenty of material.

Memphis Brooks Museum in Overton Park, 1934 Poplar Ave., 901-544-6200, brooksmuseum.org *Closed Monday and Tuesday*

Coming soon: William Eggleston continues working, shifting between Memphis and Los Angeles. Train your eye on the Eggleston Artistic Trust, directed by the photographer's son, Winston, as plans for an Eggleston museum in Memphis progress. egglestontrust.com

GET A SHELL OF A DEAL
LEVITT SHELL

What does a night of live music cost? Dinner plus parking plus tickets plus merch—if you have any money left? Not at the Levitt Shell. Thanks to a partnership with the Levitt Foundation (mission: building communities by providing free, live music), Memphis's Shell gifts you 50 free concerts a year, divided into two seasons: May through July and late August/September through October. The full schedule releases at once online, usually in March. Parking is free and you're encouraged to pack coolers/picnic baskets and blankets/chairs. Bring cash for the donation buckets or stations, and if you don't have time for a beer run, buy it onsite to benefit the Shell; food trucks usually pull up, too. As you're sitting under the stars, bewitched by the sound, consider:

Memphis's Shell was built with help from the WPA in 1936. Twenty-seven WPA-connected band shells were built nationwide around that time, but Memphis's Shell is one of the last standing.

A few weeks after Dewey Phillips, page 117, introduced Elvis Presley to his radio audience in July 1954, Elvis opened on this stage for Slim Whitman. No biggie . . . just the widely acknowledged first-ever rock-and-roll show.

The Levitt Shell is located inside Overton Park, which
is bounded by North Parkway, East Parkway, Poplar
Avenue, and McLean Boulevard, levittshell.org

· ·

HIKE AN OLD FOREST IN THE HEART OF THE CITY
OVERTON PARK'S OLD FOREST

Memphians steward Overton Park's Old Forest to the point of fighting repeatedly for it: three times culminating in a 1971 Supreme Court appeal that stopped Interstate 40 from steamrolling it, and twice recently to earn it protected status, as the Old Forest State Natural Area in 2011. At 142 acres, think of it as your personal, pocket-sized forest—smack in the middle of Memphis. Explore it on an Old Forest Nature Hike, second Saturdays and final Sundays monthly at 10 a.m., when Citizens to Preserve Overton Park guides tours. It's a different place every season, but guide Naomi Van Tol reminds that wildlife-viewing, particularly bird-watching, is productive in winter, when you're seeing only the bones of the forest. Stay warm by balancing on the giant trunks of fallen trees as you wait for the red zip of a cardinal through the forest's wintry gray and brown skeleton. Tours wind about a mile along the forest trails and average an hour depending on weather and group stamina/interest. No reservations or fees are required but donations to the park are always welcome.

The Old Forest is located inside Overton Park, which is bounded by North Parkway, East Parkway, Poplar Avenue, and McLean Boulevard, 901-299-5755, overtonparkforever.org

· ·

STAGE A SUNDAY SAFARI
MEMPHIS ZOO

Save the primates whooping and donkeys braying, Memphis Zoo keeps relatively quiet on Sunday mornings. Arrive when the gates open at 9 a.m. for uncrowded amusement, particularly in exhibits with compact displays and vantages kids vie for:

- China, where Ya Ya and Le Le make this zoo one of only four in the U.S. to house giant pandas, though the white-cheeked gibbons acrobating close by often steal the show
- Stingray Bay, available March through October for an additional $4 for non-members. On a Sunday morning, you can show up right when the exhibit opens at 9:30.
- The Herpetarium, where teeny tanks hold teeny poison dart frogs and an American alligator and alligator snapping turtle share a narrow bank
- Northwest Passage, where your kid will covet the window seat built into the polar bear pool
- Once Upon a Farm, where your kid will covet the domed look-out amid the prairie dogs

Save ample views, like elephants in the African Veldt and timber wolves in Teton Trek, for 11 a.m. and after, when daily shows and talks begin and attendance picks up.

Memphis Zoo is located inside Overton Park at
2000 Prentiss Pl., 901-333-6500, memphiszoo.org

HIP TO THIS SQUARE
OVERTON SQUARE

When a 1969 referendum legalized the sale of liquor by the drink, lore tells the license was driven directly from Nashville to Memphis's Overton Square, where Pat Halloran, page 97, swears he was among the first in line to exercise his new right. The Square caught a buzz and kept it going with a storied nightlife scene.

By the mid-1980s, the scene had migrated. But as of late 2013, it's back with so many potential tenants swirling I won't list them. Park in the new garage at 2100 Monroe Avenue or along the street by navigating to the corner of Madison Avenue and South Cooper Street. Then, walk wherever your appetite and/or shopping habit take you. In and around the Square, Bari Ristorante, Puglian authenticity with mind-blowing wine and cheese lists, and Chiwawa, Mexican, and American street food with a killer patio, hint at the variety you'll find.

Overton Square, overtonsquare.com

Bari Ristorante e Enoteca, 22 S. Cooper St., 901-722-2244,
barimemphis.com

Chiwawa, 2059 Madison Ave., 901-207-1456,
chiwawamidtown.com

GIVE A STANDING O
OVERTON SQUARE THEATERS

Just when you think you've got Overton Square figured out, the plot twists: Ta-da! You're in Memphis's theater district. In 1975, Playhouse on the Square moved in. Today, its resident professionals, plus a cast of others, star in musicals, dramas, comedies, readings, and family shows in three Overton Square venues: TheatreWorks, The Circuit, and Playhouse on the Square, which debuted its sleek structure at the corner of South Cooper Street and Union Avenue in 2010. In 2014, Memphis's black repertory theater, Hattiloo, relocated from the edge of downtown Memphis to Overton Square in a new, but intimate as ever, space. And if I say theater, you say movie, opt for four-screen Studio on the Square. The theater sells popcorn, but its beer, wine, and antipasti elevate movie munchies.

TheatreWorks, 2085 Monroe Ave., 901-274-7139,
theatreworksmemphis.org

The Circuit Playhouse, 51 S. Cooper St., 901-726-4656,
playhouseonthesquare.org

Playhouse on the Square, 66 S. Cooper St., 901-726-4656,
playhouseonthesquare.org

Hattiloo Theatre, 37 S. Cooper St., 901-525-0009, hattiloo.org

Studio on the Square, 2105 Court Ave., 901-725-7151

SCREEN. RUB ELBOWS. DRINK. REPEAT.
INDIE MEMPHIS FILM FESTIVAL

The Indie Memphis Film Festival unfolds annually over Halloween weekend. It's no Sundance, y'all—it's better. Memphis-based filmmaker Craig Brewer says that's partly because of the major studio relationships that Erik Jambor, Indie Memphis executive director, cultivates, guaranteeing that you'll see Oscar-nominated films months before they're released. Jambor credits the redevelopment of Overton Square, pages 92-93, landing six movie screens within walking distance of restaurants, bars, and a parking garage. Splice it together and you get your pick of feature films, shorts, and documentaries; Q & As with filmmakers and actors; after-parties . . . and, of course, those only-in-Memphis moments, like live music before select feature screenings and no-pretense accessibility. Prepare to line up with, pass on the street, or have drinks alongside filmmakers and actors, both the local set and those who've flown in for the event. Full festival passes give low-cost and VIP options; some single ticket options are available, too.

indiememphis.com

IN THE NEIGHBORHOOD:
EAT IN SOMEONE'S HOME (English Edition)
RESTAURANT IRIS AND THE SECOND LINE

See those fetching houses at the corner of South Cooper Street and Monroe Avenue? They aren't houses (anymore), but owner/ chef Kelly English will welcome and feed you just the same.

With advance planning—English recommends at least two weeks—reserve one of Restaurant Iris's 13 tables to taste what the fuss from *Food & Wine* and the James Beard Foundation is about. Principally, it's the French-Creole climax achieved by the ménage à trois of English's Louisiana heritage, local ingredients, and seasonal surprises.

Next door, The Second Line exposes the grit on English's chef whites, translating his upbringing on what he describes as "honest, soulful" Louisiana food, and his college days surviving on cold leftovers, into a menu of po' boys, fried Gulf seafood, smothered fries, and meat pies. Target slightly off-peak times to make the most of first-come/first-served seating in this close-packed, casual space.

Restaurant Iris, 2146 Monroe Ave., 901-590-2828,
restaurantiris.com *Closed Sunday*

The Second Line, 2144 Monroe Ave., 901-590-2829,
secondlinememphis.com

#FREEOPERA
OPERA MEMPHIS'S 30 DAYS OF OPERA

Think you hate opera? Not in Memphis you don't. Since 2012, Opera Memphis has surprised the city by popping up and belting it out at the dog park, the farmers' market, the pizza place—wherever—during its annual 30 Days of Opera series, usually planned for September. Some of the appearances are published in advance; others you'll have to crack via social media, or just listen for the trill.

Caveat: 30 Days of Opera may be something of a gateway drug, considering that Opera Memphis Director Ned Canty is the guy who reworked *The Mikado* to star Godzilla and Pikachu. You've been warned.

Oh—and if you're around in spring instead of fall, seek out the Midtown Opera Festival. Centered around Playhouse on the Square, page 93, 10 days of events include fully staged operas, world premieres of opera originals, family operas, and talks, all ticketed, plus free "fringe" events.

6745 Wolf River Pkwy., 901-257-3100, operamemphis.org

GO BACKSTAGE
(With the "Tony" Who Knows It Best)
THE ORPHEUM THEATRE

There are tons of historic and ornamental details to process at The Orpheum Theatre—literally: The Czechoslovakian chandeliers in the auditorium weigh 2,000 pounds apiece. No one knows them better than Pat Halloran, who's helmed the theater since 1980 and can talk you through its history from its origins in 1890 as the Grand Opera House. It'll cost you (around $75 for non-subscribers), but periodic Dinner on Stage events get you cocktails and a three-course meal with Halloran, plus all the personal stories you can eat. Ask Halloran about his Tony-winning work as a producer of the musical *Memphis*; then shadow him on a guided tour of the theater, which reveals 200-and-counting backstage murals created by visiting casts and crews since The Orpheum's 1996–97 season.

203 S. Main St., 901-525-3000, orpheum-memphis.com

DO BEALE BY DAY
BEALE STREET HISTORIC DISTRICT

Sure, neon lights by night are mesmerizing. But there's a quietude to Beale Street by day that's something else. Start at the Elvis statue, on Beale between South Main Street and South 2nd Street, and continue east where the Brass Note Walk of Fame memorializes music-makers from preacher/songwriters to jug bands to Justin Timberlake. Stroll into the fixture that is A. Schwab for a hoodoo souvenir and a treat from the soda fountain. Scan for historic markers (here's to you, Ida B. Wells) and don't stop 'til you've reached W.C. Handy's house, relocated from Memphis's Soulsville neighborhood, where the 20-minute guided tour is all you'll need to see where Handy lived sometime between 1905 and 1918. Today, it's trimmed with family and career photos and the air of knowing that the street and city just outside inspired classic compositions.

A. Schwab, 163 Beale St., 901-523-9782, a-schwab.com

W.C. Handy Memphis Home and Museum, 352 Beale St., 901-527-3427, wchandymemphis.org *Closed Sunday and Monday*

...AND NIGHT
BEALE STREET HISTORIC DISTRICT

On his American Dream Safari tours, Tad Pierson, page 43, steers you to blues off the beaten path. But Pierson's quick to admit, "You can't be a slouch and play on Beale." So hit Blues Hall, Rum Boogie, or the Tap Room. Keep an ear out for names like Brad Birkedahl, Eric Hughes, Ghost Town Blues Band, Jason James, and Brandon Santini slinging blues, rock-and-roll, and rockabilly. Shoot—Sundays, 6–9 p.m. at Alfred's, you can even hear the Memphis Jazz Orchestra in full swing.

Are minors allowed on Beale Street? Yes, provided you, or an adult guardian, remain with them, and only until 11 p.m. Friday and Saturday nights at 9 p.m., ID checks begin and you'll need to be 21 to come onto the street. If you're already on Beale at that time, you're all right, but mind the 11 p.m. curfew for anyone under 21.

Alfred's on Beale, 197 Beale St., 901-525-3711, alfredsonbeale.com

King's Palace Café/Tap Room, 162-168 Beale St., 901-521-1851, kingspalacecafe.com

Mr. Handy's Blues Hall/Rum Boogie Café, 182 Beale St., 901-528-0150, rumboogie.com

KNOW YOUR IBCs
INTERNATIONAL BLUES CHALLENGE AND THE BLUES FOUNDATION

The world's largest assemblage of blues acts throngs every January in downtown Memphis during the International Blues Challenge (IBC), a battle of 250 bands and solo/duo acts sponsored by affiliate blues societies worldwide. You're curious, but unsure how to break in. Let Blues Foundation President and CEO Jay Sieleman be your guide (see next page).

The Blues Foundation/IBC, 421 S. Main St., 901-527-2583, blues.org

New Daisy Theatre, 330 Beale St., 901-525-8981, newdaisy.com

The Orpheum Theatre, 203 S. Main St., 901-525-3000, orpheum-memphis.com

The IBC isn't the Blues Foundation's only gig. Since 1980, the foundation has annually inducted members into a Blues Hall of Fame. The recordings and biographical sketches are all there; what's missing is the hall. Cue the capital campaign: Construction begins in 2014 to retrofit the foundation's South Main Street offices with public space for exhibiting those recordings, original art, photos, film, and artifacts.

"Go Tuesday, Wednesday or Saturday [of IBC] without battling crowds."

Tuesday night, the New Daisy Theatre traditionally hosts IBC's International Showcase. Wednesday marks the first—read: quieter—night of the quarterfinals at clubs along Beale Street. Saturday, The Orpheum Theatre hosts the finals, "so you don't have to jump from club to club," Sieleman adds.

"Thursday [night two of the quarterfinals] and Friday [the semifinals] are the busiest on the streets and in the clubs."

The Blues Foundation sells a pass that gets you into all IBC events, or you can go à la carte: Buy wristbands on Beale Street for IBC access Wednesday through Friday; buy individual tickets from the New Daisy and/or The Orpheum for their respective events.

PARTY ALL MAY LONG
MEMPHIS IN MAY
INTERNATIONAL FESTIVAL

Memphis in May International Festival began in 1977 as a cultural exchange between Memphis and the world. Today, it's a month-long multicultural party stoked famously by Beale Street Music Festival and the World Championship Barbecue Cooking Contest, both detailed on the following pages. Don't let these heavies overshadow smaller-scale demonstrations of visual art, music, theater, and dance happening every May across Memphis, each one illuminating the festival's honored country.

memphisinmay.org

PACK YOUR WELLIES
BEALE STREET MUSIC FESTIVAL

Beale Street Music Festival (BSMF), held annually the first weekend in May, is big. Big as in hordes of fans counting down to its lineup announcement, usually in February. Big as in five stages, 70-plus acts and thousands of attendees. Big as in past performers Joan Jett and Snoop Dogg. And big on rolling with whatever the weather deals—rain, mud—it all adds to the experience. If you're studying Memphis music, the fest can help you cram: I saw Jerry Lee Lewis for the first time at the festival, and though I've been spoiled seeing my favorite home-honed act, Lucero, on small stages, I won't pass up the chance to see them perform before the crowds here. BSMF also provides a ready-made stage for Memphis rappers like Juicy J. For a fest-within-a-fest feel, steal inside the Blues Tent.

BSMF takes place in Tom Lee Park along Riverside Drive in downtown Memphis, memphisinmay.org/musicfestival

SNIFF OUT THE WORLD CHAMPIONSHIP BARBECUE COOKING CONTEST

Annually, the World Championship Barbecue Cooking Contest (WCBCC) draws around 250 internationally seeded teams competing in categories like ribs, whole hog, and wings. Then, thousands of people smell it cooking and follow. Go ahead and mark your calendar for the third weekend in May. Just don't be the one who shows up ignorant of the cardinal rule: Teams may not serve the general public (health regulations). Still, there are ways to savor the experience; see the next page.

WCBCC takes place in Tom Lee Park along Riverside Drive in downtown Memphis, memphisinmay.org/worldchampionshipbbqcontest

Join the **Cooker's Caravan**, a free, guided tour featuring teams who talk you through their cookers and methods. The tours are typically given at regular mid-day intervals Thursday and Friday of WCBCC.

Register in advance for the **Kingsford Tour of Champions**. For around $10, you'll taste samples prepared by select teams; then vote for your favorite.

To **build a relationship with a team**, target daytime Thursday or Friday of the contest. Rodney Ashley, cook for the Paradise Porkers, suggests: "Ask a cook about his or her cooker. They all want to show off, and they might even bring you in and give you a sample."

For a visual feast, wander. Teams construct booths where they live and work throughout the contest, booths that might be one or three stories high and incorporate tiki bars or animatronic dinosaurs. General admission to WCBCC, usually less than $10 and free mid-day Thursday and Friday of the contest, buys you all the gawking you want.

CIRCUIT THESE FESTIVALS
MUSIC FESTS WITH INTIMATE SCENES AND UNFORGETTABLE SOUNDS

Looking for a music showcase you won't have to share with thousands of your closest friends? Try one on the next page.

Gonerfest

As a label, Goner Records embodies what owners Eric Friedl and Zac Ives like, self-described as "eclectic with a live energy that comes across on a record." Gonerfest, sounding off annually in late September, puts 40 relevant acts, some local, some international, on Midtown Memphis stages. Pile up for free opening and closing shows at the Cooper-Young gazebo across the street from Goner Records, page 71. Past performers: Ex-Cult, Guitar Wolf, True Sons of Thunder.

goner-records.com/gonerfest

Memphis Music & Heritage Festival

A true genre-bender where you're as likely to hear gospel as garage rock and see someone jookin' or beat-boxin'. Unfolds annually on Labor Day weekend inside the Center for Southern Folklore, page 108, and along the South Main Street mall. Past performers: Susan Marshall, Bobby Rush, Tav Falco's Panther Burns.

southernfolklore.com

Rock for Love

This annual benefit for Memphis's Church Health Center doubles as an orientation to some of the city's most accessible acts in some of its most accessible venues. Around the second weekend in September, watch for free, signature performances on Midtown Memphis streets and at the Levitt Shell, page 89. Past performers: Dead Soldiers, Kirk Whalum, The Memphis Dawls.

rockforlove.org

CENTER YOURSELF
CENTER FOR SOUTHERN FOLKLORE

If you haven't been to the Center for Southern Folklore, I'll forgive you. But you darn sure better get there before I ask you again.

The Center leads something of a double life: Its vivid, sound-soaked party space fronts an ambitious mission to preserve Delta culture. Center co-founder Judy Peiser's been at it since 1972, gathering audio, films, and photographs of Southern crafters, farmers, and musicians.

Back to the party: At an age most would fade into retirement, Peiser's still staying up late, passing around a tip jar for the acts she books most Friday and Saturday nights. Her bookings give credence to every musical expression from throwback sounds to contemporary currents, though friends of the Center make repeat and memorable appearances, Daddy Mack Blues Band, J Train, and Randall Morton among them. The common thread: Peiser puts artists on stage who tell a story through their music.

So go. Pay the nominal cover charge. Order a beer or greens and cornbread or cobbler. Put something in the tip jar for the performers, and buy one of their CDs, or a little chunk of folk art, a vintage concert bill, or a photo from the Center's archive. The Center's put me onto some of my favorite bands to follow around town. I promise it'll do the same for you.

123 S. Main St., 901-525-3655, southernfolklore.com

● ●

STALK THIS BAND
SONS OF MUDBOY

Mudboy and the Neutrons, though active for decades and heavily influential, was a tough act to pin down live. And by summer 2013, founding members Lee Baker, Jim Dickinson, and Sid Selvidge had passed away. But their sons, Ben Baker, Cody and Luther Dickinson, and Steve Selvidge, along with surviving "Mudboy" Jimmy Crosthwait and supporting musicians, come together on rare occasions as Sons of Mudboy. The challenge is chasing the occasions. Wait for the brothers Dickinson to come in off the road with North Mississippi Allstars, and for Selvidge to break from touring with The Hold Steady. Like facebook.com/SonsOfMudboy. Watch the event calendar for Minglewood Hall; past appearances have turned up at the venue's 1884 Lounge. Then, come out and listen to the legacy.

Minglewood Hall, 1555 Madison Ave., 901-312-6058, minglewoodhall.com

AIN'T NO JAM LIKE A SUPER-GROUP JAM
MEMPHIS-BASED SUPER-GROUPS

As a Memphian, I sometimes feel like the steady partner in a wandering relationship—my other half being the musicians I'm attached to. They'll leave you for tours and return restless. On the flipside, their talent and drive to perform breeds an inimitable super-group culture, mixing and matching musicians into a sure thing every time. You're bound to encounter at least one of the following while you're in town; for appearances, check the websites listed or *Memphis Flyer,* free in stands citywide and at memphisflyer.com.

Bluff City Backsliders

Amid the barrelhouse banjos, fiddles, and mandolins, look for Jason Freeman on lead and Victor Sawyer on trombone.

bluffcitybacksliders.bandcamp.com

The City Champs

An instrumental trio that picks up where Booker T. Jones left off on his organ.

facebook.com/TheCityChamps

Hope Clayburn's Soul Scrimmage

The only woman I know who can play two saxophones at once, with filmmaker Rob Parker on guitar and Paul Taylor on drums.

hopeclayburn.com

Mighty Souls Brass Band

This stage full of brass includes saxophonist Jim Spake when he's not on the road with Lucero, and jazzy Jeremy Shrader on trumpet.

mightysoulsbrassband.com

BRUNCH WITH "THE WALKING JUKEBOX"
JOYCE COBB AT BOSCOS SQUARED

Joyce Cobb moved to Memphis in the 1970s when Jim Stewart signed her to a country-western recording contract with Volt, a subsidiary of Stax Records, page 44, right before the studio closed. We're glad she stayed. Though her influence echoes all around—hear her spinning world music on WEVL FM 89.9 or teaching jazz vocals at the University of Memphis—Cobb's notes go down smooth with Sunday Brunch at Boscos Squared (11 a.m.–3 p.m.). For 14 years, she's been singing from the book of American pop standards at the restaurant, now with a multipiece band that might include fiddle, saxophone, and flute. For its part, Boscos's brunch menu performs variations on the bloody mary, bellini, and mimosa.

2120 Madison Ave., 901-432-2222, boscosbeer.com

CONTEMPLATE:
IS IT THE FOOD? THE DRINKS? THE SPACE? THE MUSIC?
KAREN CARRIER'S RESTAURANTS AND BARS

Karen Carrier's restaurants and bars—Mollie Fontaine Lounge, The Beauty Shop Restaurant + Lounge, and Bar DKDC—serve up cocktails and sharing plates that know how to be whimsical *and* well done. And each concept occupies a space that takes "sense of place" to the edge: Mollie Fontaine in a circa-1886 Eclectic Revival home; The Beauty Shop, where Priscilla Presley had her beehives done—request the first booth on the left from the bar to sit in the exact spot; Bar DKDC next door, bathed in shadowy hues. If that isn't enough, Carrier commonly books Memphis's beloved talents at Bar DKDC and Mollie Fontaine. Listen for Motel Mirrors, the Amy LaVere/John Paul Keith collaboration, Lee Taylor's torch songs, and the *je ne sais quoi* of Marcella Simien, winner of a 2014 Grammy.

Bar DKDC, 964 S. Cooper St., 901-272-0830,
bardkdc.com *Closed Sunday and Monday*

Mollie Fontaine Lounge, 679 Adams Ave., 901-524-1886,
molliefontainelounge.com *Closed Sunday through Tuesday*

The Beauty Shop Restaurant + Lounge, 966 S. Cooper St.,
901-272-7111, thebeautyshoprestaurant.com

STEEP IN
COFFEEHOUSE CULTURE
OTHERLANDS COFFEE BAR

Otherlands Coffee Bar is where you go when you want more out of your coffee than a lip-lock with a paper cup. It's coffeehouse culture: that neighborhood gathering spot where your espresso comes in a mismatched mug, a cozy den pulls you in to read or chat, and weekend nights fetch live music (suggested listening: Harlan T. Bobo, Cory Branan, Dan Montgomery). These Otherlands Live shows are all-ages and smoke-free; they're also first-come/first-served. Bring cash for cover and join the Otherlands Live Facebook group for dates. Otherlands also serves breakfast, lunch, beer, and free Wi-Fi, but I'm partial to the cookies, bars, and muffins at the cash wrap; vegan options included. Otherlands's back deck is also a lively place to congregate.

641 S. Cooper St., 901-278-4994, otherlandscoffeebar.com

SHOP SHANGRI-LA RECORDS

Buy or sell; new or used; vinyl or CD: Shangri-La Records entertains it all in that brown house on Madison Avenue, but you can bet the Memphis section (sections, rather) are loaded. So go on: Hunt for that rare Furry Lewis. Build your Big Star collection. Ransack the local bestsellers at the register for classic Al Green or new Mark Edgar Stuart. Let curiosity best you and ask for a look at what's rare—perhaps *Stay in School*, Stax's limited 1967 release interspersing hits with PSAs by Eddie Floyd and Sam & Dave. Don't be afraid to ask anyone behind the counter for guidance: Ever ready with recommendations, they're musicians themselves, including guitarist/vocalist J.D. Reager and Wuvbirds guitarist Jared McStay, who moonlights as Shangri-La's owner.

1916 Madison Ave., 901-274-1916, shangri.com

JOIN THE CARAVAN
BEALE STREET CARAVAN RADIO SHOW

Here's one you can do from anywhere in the world: Tune into Beale Street Caravan, the weekly, hour-long radio broadcast of Memphis music and its "derivative forms" to three million-plus listeners across the globe. Define derivative? "If we can connect the dots to Memphis, that's a story we need to tell," explains Caravan Executive Producer Kevin Cubbins, and so the series swings from blues to folk to gospel to rock-and-roll to roots to soul and so on, as performed by music-makers based in Memphis and beyond. Cubbins's crew records at concerts and festivals across the U.S. to present two acts per broadcast, and weekly guest spots can be just as powerful: Listen for personalities like Ardent Studios's producer/engineer Adam Hill, who might show up to chat about recording ZZ Top in Memphis, or anything else he's working on. Visit the Caravan's website to learn where and when to listen, and to find archived broadcasts.

bealestreetcaravan.com

SEE DADDY-O DEWEY'S BOOTH
AT SUN STUDIO

When redevelopment of Memphis's Hotel Chisca began recently, Sun Studio employees hustled to save what they could of Dewey Phillips's DJ booth. They salvaged elements—acoustic tiles from the ceiling and walls, floors, control room glass—and reassembled them on the second floor of Sun Studio in 2014, 60 years after Phillips used the booth to introduce Elvis Presley to his radio audience. Moral of the story: If it's been awhile since you've toured Sun Studio, here's your reason to return. If you've never toured Sun Studio, it's high time to see the humble space that materialized explosive dreams. It's not a dull spot to order a milkshake either, surrounded by all those records and photos of the Million Dollar Quartet, Howlin' Wolf, and Rufus Thomas, catchy soundtrack playing all the while. Tours are available for visitors ages 5 and up daily, 10 a.m.–6 p.m. on the bottom half of the hour.

706 Union Ave., 800-441-6249, sunstudio.com

EXPERIENCE GRACELAND ON ANY BUDGET

Graceland is one of the most visited homes in the U.S. In other words, Elvis Presley Enterprises doesn't need my help convincing you to visit. Yet some of you are reading this insisting Graceland isn't for you. I hear you, and I raise you:

"Been there; done that." Yay for you. But know that exhibits in and around the mansion change regularly, so you might see something new, like the *60 Years of Elvis* exhibit that debuted on the Entourage VIP Tour in 2014.

"I'm not an Elvis fan." Maybe not, but I bet you like the Beatles or James Brown or Bruce Springsteen or Katy Perry, just a few of the artists who claim Elvis as an inspiration.

"I'm on a budget." While you're saving up for that Entourage VIP Tour, you can do loads for free or just a few bucks. "During Elvis Week [annually in mid-August], there's the official list of activities and the unofficial," Memphis music tour guide Mike Freeman told me, right before sharing these word-of-mouth to-dos that'll give you the feel of Elvis Week without demanding a hunk o' cash (see the next page).

Graceland, 3734 Elvis Presley Blvd., 901-332-3322, elvis.com

Mike's Memphis Tours, 901-289-7401, mikesmemphistours.com

Clarion Hotel Airport/Graceland

A tradeshow stuffs two ballrooms with memorabilia and records, plus free tribute performances.

1471 E. Brooks Rd., 901-332-3500

Rock & Roll Café strip mall

Take in the free musical tent show pitched in the parking lot.

3717 Elvis Presley Blvd., #5, 901-398-5692

Marlowe's Ribs & Restaurant

Time drinks or dinner with one of the many free tribute shows that roll through the restaurant during Elvis Week. "It's like getting Elvis Week for the cost of a beer," Freeman nudges.

4381 Elvis Presley Blvd., 901-332-4159, marlowesmemphis.com

Note, too, that annually on the night of August 15, the gates of Graceland open for free to anyone wishing to participate in the Candlelight Vigil. The procession usually lasts into the morning of August 16, the anniversary of Elvis's death. Parking is free, too. And any time of year, taking a photo starring those gates costs nothing; nor does a tiptoe up the driveway to the Meditation Garden, available most days of the year, 7:30 to 8:30 a.m.

DON'T BE A KNOW-IT-ALL
MEMPHIS ROCK 'N' SOUL MUSEUM

You've been to Stax, Sun, and Graceland and think you know all there is to know about Memphis music. You don't. But the Memphis Rock 'n' Soul Museum will connect the dots, tracing Robert Johnson to Eric Clapton, Jimmie Lunceford to the Cotton Club, and so on. The playlist alone at this Smithsonian-curated institution makes it worth a visit, and when you're ready, you can take your field trip to the streets with an audio walking tour of Beale. This is Beale like Beale can't even show you: Numbered stops on a souvenir map conjure a time when orchestras filled these clubs, blues acts filled the streets, and W.C. Handy, page 98, found inspiration inside Pee Wee's Saloon. Keep the headset for the day, pausing for lunch or anything else. An $18 combo gives you museum admission and the audio walking tour, or take the tour à la carte for $10.

191 Beale St., #100, 901-205-2533, memphisrocknsoul.org

STICK AROUND AFTER THE DUCK MARCH
THE PEABODY MEMPHIS

Daily at 11 a.m. and 5 p.m., five North American mallards waddle down a red carpet and splash into the fabled lobby fountain of The Peabody Memphis, very much like they have since 1933. Arrive early and stay late: Crowds begin gathering by 10:30 a.m., so the earlier you show, the better your chance of scoring a table, a photo with the Duckmaster, and a bloody mary. Kids, don't be shy about sitting right on the edge of the red carpet, or asking the Duckmaster for a keepsake lapel pin. Following the procession, march yourself to the concierge desk to reserve a spot on the 11:30 a.m. history tour ($5 for hotel guests; $10 for the public). The Duckmaster himself leads this hour-long junket, spilling with stories of Tommy Dorsey and his orchestra playing the Skyway Ballroom; Vernon Presley and son signing Elvis's first RCA contract, on view in the hotel's Memorabilia Room; and "secret" architectural details (the lobby's faux skylight abounds with chestnuts).

149 Union Ave., 901-529-4000, peabodymemphis.com

...AND END ON
A SWEET NOTE
THE PEABODY MEMPHIS

People-watching at The Peabody has been a thing at least as long ago as 1935, when historian David Cohn threw out that bit about the Mississippi Delta beginning in the hotel's lobby. Indulge in the tableau with live piano music, 5–10 p.m. nightly, and anything from the dessert cart. Created by The Peabody's Executive Pastry Chef Konrad Spitzbart and team, each selection resembles a tiny present tempting you to unwrap it, like the tiramisu cradled in a chocolate tass. If it's a nightcap you're craving, know that every bottle of Jack Daniel's Single Barrel Select Tennessee Whiskey poured at The Peabody is handpicked by hotel staff, and bartenders are just as carefully trained in case your beverage of choice is mixed, muddled, or infused with fresh-squeezed juice.

149 Union Ave., 901-529-4000, peabodymemphis.com

SUGGESTED ITINERARIES

ACTIVE/OUTDOORS

CLASSIC

FOODIE

FREE

• •

HISTORY

MUSIC ATTRACTIONS AND TOURS

NIGHT OUT

WITH KIDS

ACTIVITIES
BY SEASON

WINTER

Bird-watch in the Old Forest, 90

Elvis Presley's Birthday Celebration at Graceland, 118

International Blues Challenge, 100

St. Jude Memphis Marathon Weekend, 77

EARLY SPRING

Broad Avenue Spring Art Walk, 69

Farmers' market season opens, 9, 26

Ghost River Rentals season opens (paddle the Wolf River), 79

Jimmy Ogle Bridge Walks begin, 38

Meeman-Shelby Forest State Park, 81

Memphis Redbirds baseball season opens, 86

Memphis Riverboats season opens, 33

Midtown Opera Festival, 96

Mud Island River Park season opens, 32

Old Millington Winery concert series begins, 16

LATE SPRING

EARLY SUMMER

LATE SUMMER

Central Gardens Association Home & Garden Tour, 54
Elvis Week, 118
Memphis Music & Heritage Festival, 107
Rock for Love, 107

FALL

30 Days of Opera, 96
Broad Avenue Fall Art Walk, 69
Cooper-Young Regional Beerfest, 13
Elmwood Cemetery Twilight Tour, 48
Gonerfest, 107
Indie Memphis, 94
Jimmy Ogle Bridge Walks resume, 38
Levitt Shell concert series resumes, 89
Old Millington Winery concert series resumes, 16
Repair Days at the Metal Museum, 37

● ●

HELPFUL LINKS

- **TNVacation.com/triptales** New ideas from me weekly to help you explore more of Memphis.

- **MemphisTravel.com** Planning tools including a mobile app for use when you're in town and free downloads of the annual visitor guide, plus daily updates on what to do and where to eat at **ilovememphisblog.com**.

INDEX

• •

• •

• •

• •